"Honest and humorous, poignant and practical, and packed with biblical truth that will encourage singles to embrace God's plan for their lives. Highly recommended."

Marlene Bagnull, Write His Answer Ministries

"In a world that may paint the picture that every Christian woman should be married and have a family, Alisha's honest confessions and experience remind us that may not be the reality of God's plan and will for every woman's life. With helpful questions and practical tools along the way, Alisha encourages us that relationship with God is the highest priority and that He has a purpose and a plan to use every one of His daughters (single or married) in mighty ways."

Linnea Sandvall, Awana missionary and author

"Beyond being relevant for single adult women, Plummer's readable, insightful, accessible prose should become a must-read for every pastor and minister to single adults. She tells her story and bares her heart about her unmarried journey with witty, vulnerable, transparent, and focused ease. She traverses beyond the hard, sometimes awkward questions about singleness into weighty matters of daily living with God in divine fellowship and maturity. As a medical practitioner, she deals forthrightly and biblically with sex, sexual desires, and sexual perversions. Her thought-provoking approach to relationships and the church is biblically driven and inherently practical. Plummer rightly reflects on the need for people—everyone, not just singles—to focus on becoming the whole person God made them to become. No one's 'other half' lurks somewhere waiting to complete them; God made every believer to be whole in Him. Plummer explains that reality deftly. Enjoyable. Recommended."

Dr. Kevin Parker, pastor, denominational communications director, Baptist Convention of New Mexico

CONFESSIONS

OF A CHRISTIAN

SPINSTER

CONFESSIONS

OF A CHRISTIAN

SPINSTER

Finding Purpose in a Perplexed and Paired-Up Church

ALISHA PLUMMER

KREGEL
PUBLICATIONS

Confessions of a Christian Spinster: Finding Purpose in a Perplexed and Paired-Up Church
© 2023 by Alisha Plummer

Published by Kregel Publications, a division of Kregel Inc., 2450 Oak Industrial Dr. NE, Grand Rapids, MI 49505. www.kregel.com.

Cataloging-in-Publication Data is available from the Library of Congress.

ISBN 978-0-8254-4803-4, print
ISBN 978-0-8254-7082-0, epub
ISBN 978-0-8254-6981-7, Kindle

Printed in the United States of America
23 24 25 26 27 28 29 30 31 32 / 5 4 3 2 1

Dedicated to Christ's church and His kingdom

CONTENTS

Contents

Confessions of the Flesh

Confessions of the Soul

ACKNOWLEDGMENTS

To my long-suffering and supportive family, thank you. To my mother and my brother, Josiah, who have graciously read everything I ever asked them to, thank you. To my beta readers, Judy, Dan, Lynda, and Angie, who were so encouraging with their comments and suggestions, thank you. To Jenn, who was instrumental in several aspects of *Confessions*, thank you. To my photographer, Elena, who was graciously willing and flexible, thank you. And, Lord, for the life, relationships, and gifts You have given me, thank You doesn't cut it, but I am so grateful.

INTRODUCTION

I FREELY CONFESS: I AM a freak of the natural world and a freak of the spiritual world.

I am a Christian in her thirties, not married, and always back in the singles Sunday school class like a boomerang. Churches have had no idea what to do with me, and for years, neither did I. I didn't fit in anywhere. I didn't feel integral to the purpose or the passion of the church. My singleness wasn't a blessing—it was a ball and chain ensuring a meaningless life for me. Perhaps you relate to my freakish status (maybe rather painfully), and if you do, you may agree that being unattached can be devastating. For years, my relationship status was the worst part of my life . . . until God painstakingly reshaped my heart to grasp the truths of His world and Word.

I am loved. I belong. I am useful. I am His. And so are you.

Unlike today's church and church members, God is not mystified that singles sit in the pews. Not even close. He has masterful purposes for those of us who lack husbands. Perpetually single or single again after death, divorce, or the dissolution of a courting or dating relationship, no matter your circumstance, the Lord invites each one of us, His daughters, to rise up and seize our place.

The confessions you are about to read are an exposé on Christian singleness inspired by personal experiences but rooted in the truth of God's Word rather than in my perception of my circumstances. Together we will enjoy humorous tales and connect with each other through the trials of singleness. We will explore God's vision and design for Christian singles. We will be encouraged and challenged to seek out our role in Christ's kingdom. And incrementally we will engage with our calling from God to receive His peace, stand firm in our faith, and live single-mindedly for His everlasting kingdom.

There are four sections. "Confessions of the Heart" deals with the emotional questions and struggles of living as God's single. "Confessions of the Mind" builds a godly perspective of Christian singleness. "Confessions of the Flesh" discusses how to be victorious over temptations, both obvious and less obvious. "Confessions of the Soul" addresses doubts, worries, and how to live by faith.

At the close of each confession is a special time to reflect on what the Holy Spirit is teaching you and to pray. This quiet moment with your Savior culminates in "Take a Single Step," a practical opportunity to apply the truths of God's Word to your life, ministry, and relationships.

Even though my interpretation of Christian singleness may not be representative of every single, my prayer is that it will still be informative, instructive, and entertaining. I hope you will find yourself nodding, laughing, crying (if that is where you are, there is no shame), and most of all hearing God's still, small voice. May you become convinced you are not alone and your singleness has purpose. Those are not my promises. (If they were, what value would they have?) They are God's promises.

So from me to you, enjoy *Confessions of a Christian Spinster*. May you be able to read with your eyes, your heart, and your mouth wide open in laughter and aha moments . . . and maybe before the end, you'll have a few confessions of your own to add.

In Christ and for His glory,

Alisha

CONFESSIONS

OF THE

HEART

He who trusts in his own heart is a fool,
But whoever walks wisely will be delivered.

PROVERBS 28:26

Confession 1

IT'S NOT LIKE BEING PICKED LAST

CHRISTIAN SINGLES ARE UNICORNS. WE are beautiful but unique to the point of being shocking. We've all heard the whispers: Is that really what a unicorn looks like? We are gifted, but no one is sure if we belong in the herd. Can a unicorn truly fit in with horses? We are rare, even arguably mythical. Where do unicorns come from anyway? Well . . .

"Hidden on the highest mountains and lost in the lowest valleys, is where unicorns are born." Jane's teacher began his story. "A unicorn's parents aren't unicorns—they are horses. So unicorns are born looking just like any other horse. Until one day when they are nearly mares or stallions, a nub appears between their eyes. Slowly the nub loses its hair, hardens, and sharpens into a beautiful spiral horn."

"What color?" Jane didn't raise her hoof.

The wise horse shrugged. "Only God knows—but every unicorn horn is different and beautiful."

"Ugh." One of Jane's classmates shuddered. "How horrible to have a big stick in the middle of your face."

"Oh no. It's not horrible." The teacher smiled. "Unicorns are one in a million. They have special jobs only they can do."

"But what about the things they can't be? And the things they can't do?" Jane made up her mind. "I think it's better just to be like everyone else."

The teacher leaned closer. "But if you are like everyone else, Jane, who will be who God made you to be?"

🐉

I was not thinking about who God wanted me to be when one of my bosses suddenly blurted, "You strike me as someone who would like to be married and have kids."

"I would." I didn't hesitate. But what I didn't say was I was nearly desperate. I merely shrugged. "God hasn't brought the right man yet."

"You know," he said after ten seconds, "there's this man at my church. He's a nurse and an all-around great guy. I could invite him over. I think you both have a lot in common."

Saying anything here, I had learned, was counterproductive. You would either offend the person who'd made the kind offer to set you up or give the impression you were chomping at the bit. Fortunately, break time was over. My boss moved on to something else, and we forgot about it.

Or at least I did, until a clean-cut young man arrived for a tour of my office building and to go out to lunch with some coworkers and me.

I'll save you the question. He enjoyed his tour, and I enjoyed getting out of my basement office. But there were no sparks between us—and a different kind of sparks came later, over pizza.

Prospective boyfriend included, there were five of us at lunch. The last-minute addition was an unmarried male coworker who, I was informed later, had a crush on me.

The pizza was fine, but any spontaneous, three-way, blind group date is bound to go poorly. And it did. Thank goodness it was short.

But not short enough to keep the two young men from competing with each other, trying to protect their turf and attempting to figure out the other's intentions. All with me caught in the middle.

As we walked back to the office, my friend said, "You know, our boss asked him to come down here just to meet you."

Now I admit, I can be a bit dim-witted at times, but I'm not dense. Afraid to say too much, I chose the frank approach. "I did know." I smiled and never heard from either young man romantically again. Maybe I wasn't worth fighting over.

Remember when we were kids, how we lined up for kickball, dodgeball, and just about every other team sport? The most athletic boys were team captains, and the good players were selected first, until only mediocre or poor players were left. I often was the last one waiting, but it never really bothered me. I just wanted the chance to play, even if I was the last one picked.

Being a spinster is not like being picked last. It is like not being picked at all. We stood in line, waiting as patiently as we could. We prepared to play the game as much as (and maybe more than) everyone else. Then they paired off to play, and we—the unicorns—were left standing there, alone, unchosen.

In a hotly debated passage, God says bluntly, "Jacob I have loved, but Esau I have hated" (Romans 9:13).

God chose Jacob and the people of Israel as His servants (Luke 1:54) to display His glory among all the nations (Psalm 96:3). He dwelt among them as the Lord (Exodus 29:43–46) and poured His everlasting love out on them (Jeremiah 31:3). At the same time, though Esau and the Edomites were given a specific inheritance (Deuteronomy 2:5), they were not chosen as God's special people.

Romans 9:13 is easy for a single Christian woman to understand— we've seen it played out over and over in daily life. This Sunday the guy who always sits in front of me brought his girlfriend to church.

He chose her—Jacob I have loved. He could have, but didn't, choose me—Esau I have hated. Does he love her? I don't know, but in comparison to me, yes. Does he hate me? No, but in comparison to her, yes.

Being chosen is so irreplaceably special that it's easy to be confused by being unchosen and to read into our singlehood things neither God nor others intend. I couldn't even begin to guess at the number of times I have asked myself, What is wrong with me? I like me. Why don't men like me? Am I not pretty enough? Not thin enough? Not flirtatious enough? Am I too smart? Too serious? Too old-fashioned?

Then the questions get ugly. Why does she get what I want? (The assumption being I am better than her.)

What am I doing wrong? (The assumption being if I am doing things "right," I will get what I want.)

Why am I not worthy of being a wife? (The assumption is that marriage is the ultimate evidence of value.)

Why haven't I been chosen? (The assumption is that being chosen by God doesn't count.)

And after the questions get ugly, the conclusions have no chance of being logical or intellectual. Instead, they become a mass of unpredictable, raw emotions.

These are emotions that have left me—and maybe you as well—crying on the bathroom floor so intensely I nearly pass out. They leave me blind with rage. *Why did God do this to me? Clearly one of us made a mistake somewhere, and it wasn't me. Where am I supposed to go now? My dreams for life are destroyed.* This grief can be overwhelming, as I mourn the loss of what I never had. And these emotions leave me simmering in frustration, thinking, *This is what my obedience to God got me.*

But no matter what you might feel as a Christian spinster, you get up every Sunday and smile. You pretend everything is okay—because it's unspiritual to be in the depths of despair over love. And everything truly is going well . . . except you aren't getting what you really want out of life.

Oh sure, you might bring it up once or twice in conversation, but eventually you just push it down. Because most people are married and think they understand, but they don't. Even people who really love you don't know if your singleness will ever change. And you are afraid everyone else will be awakened to those questions you have about yourself, so it's easier not to open the door to any subject that might lead to those questions.

Married or not, everyone has felt that sting of being the last choice, being left out, or being rejected. Rarely is it completely true, but that doesn't stop us from feeling that way. Feelings are real. And they motivate real choices, everything from joining a nunnery to hanging out at bars.

It is tempting (and oh so easy) to wallow in our self-pity—some of us have more than enough justification. But that choice elevates what I feel over what God says is true. Self-pity cuts us off from hearing and obeying God's voice because we have actively decided to follow our own heart instead of God's.

The truth is, even if I am never picked, even if you are never picked, we were not created to follow our hearts. We were made to follow after God's heart. We have been chosen as the bride of Christ, and God says, "Jacob, Alisha, [your name here], I have loved you."

REFLECT

How do you feel about your singleness? Why do you feel this way?

PRAY

Tell God how you feel about being unmarried. Confused? Content? Hurt? Happy? Angry? Apathetic? No matter how you feel, you can be honest before God without feeling guilty. Your Savior knows, understands, and has a beautiful future for you.

TAKE A SINGLE STEP

Write yourself a love note from God using His words in Scripture. Some passages that may resonant with you include Psalm 16; Psalm 145; Romans 8:31–39; Ephesians 1:3–14; and 1 Peter 1:3–9.

Confession 2

THE MAKING OF A CHRISTIAN SPINSTER

WE ALL HAVE OUR OWN wild story behind why we are single. Our stories are different, but in every one God is there. Even in the most heartbreaking tales and zaniest situations, our Lord is at work in the lives of His daughters.

A cool evening breeze blew as my sister, neighbor, and I hiked into the wilderness near our neighborhood. On our way back to civilization, we ran into a middle school boy.

He engaged us in playful conversation and managed to ask all of us, at least once, if we wanted to go out with him. But as the youngest-looking of the group, he honed in on me. (I was the oldest, but for about fifteen years, I looked like I was fifteen years old.) So I was the one who got to gently tell him no at least three times, while trying to avoid the awkward conversation that begins with either "do you know what statutory rape is?" or "I am almost old enough to be your mother."

This wasn't a onetime problem. Later that semester, a different middle schooler accused me of being her classmate. And while I was working at the state capitol, a high school chaperone scolded me for not keeping up with the field trip. Thus, I present the following.

Contention 1: My persistent teenage appearance (I think it's the acne) is definitely God's fault, and it has kept me from being pursued by suitors.

Regardless of what people think, it's hard not looking your age. I am the only one I know who is excited their wrinkles are starting to show. For years men my age glossed over me, assuming I was a child—to their credit. And the (very) young men who were interested lost interest when they realized I could buy cigarettes, could own firearms, and was nearing age eligibility to become president of the United States.

Contention 2: My family (who is also God's fault) has kept me away from suitors.

It started with my dad, a marine and a high-ranking military officer. This not only led to frequent moves, but eligible young men avoided my father's daughters like the plague because fraternization regulations and court-martialing were (and are) still a thing.

But perhaps worst of all, once my youngest brother grew facial hair, people assumed we were dating or married. Which is a compliment to me because I am eleven years older, and an insult to him.

Contention 3: My Bible has kept me from pursuing a suitor because God says, "Trust in Me with all your heart and lean not on your own understanding."

The summer before tenth grade, I went to a conference in Arizona. There I heard the story of an eighteen-year-old girl in the audience, listening to a single twenty-eight-year-old guy speak. Near the end of his sermon, she felt that she was supposed to marry him. Not only that, she felt convicted that God wanted her to approach this man and propose. So she did. He said yes. And they were married and now have two kids.

Sitting there on my spiritual high, I told myself I would obey if God asked me to do that.

But truthfully, I am not sure if I would have. The good news is that as much as I may have wanted to, I never heard God say, "Go propose to that man." Instead, I was tasked with something arguably harder: "Wait on the Lord."

So I did. I resisted the urge to act on my crushes when I was young. I had to reject the temptation to give in to my desperation when I was . . . less young. And I slowly received God's grace to live a single life to glorify Him.

Conclusion: It is God's fault I am a spinster.

Yes, I am serious. But even if I have made mistakes in love (which is almost certain), and even if I missed "the one" He had for me because of my stubbornness (which is certainly possible), I know my Redeemer is mighty. He will not allow my sin to overshadow His claim on my life. Jesus will perform a great work in me and through me, using my mistakes, my gifts, and, yes, my singleness.

But honestly, coming from my background and my family, not being married could easily be devastating. I never wanted this.

Eight months before I was born (I was a month early), I started attending church and never stopped. That immersion in the truth of God's Word is a blessing I wouldn't trade for anything. The family atmosphere of Christ's church is inviting and full of hope for the future, personally and for the kingdom of God.

I grew up in those comfy pews watching mothers, old and young, and waiting and preparing for the day when I would join them. As the oldest of four children, I got a fair amount of practice. And when it comes to anything homemaking, I can compete with the best of them. Proverbs 31 was embedded in my mind before I reached double digits. I knew all the biblical passages dealing with womanhood, marriage, and family by heart.

Everyone assumed I would marry a great Christian guy, have a close brood of children, minister together as a family, and, of course, homeschool.

That was the ideal, consciously and subconsciously, presented everywhere for Christian girls who loved and served God. Once in a while someone would dare whisper there were a few people whom God would call to be single. But this was a remote possibility—hardly worth discussing since it wouldn't happen to very many of us. (So I guess I could be considered lucky.)

High school came and went without any serious prospects. I delayed college, secretly thinking, *Maybe this is the time for "him" to come.* When *he* was not forthcoming, I went to college, but under protest because I was still dreaming the four-point dream above. College was quickly over, and God opened the door to graduate school, but I still wanted a husband and a home. So I established myself in my profession, hanging on to my dream by a thread.

And that's when I realized as Christian spinsters, we are designed to pursue God and His ways, and as a result, we haven't practiced skills to attract or retain men. At the same time, we often have abilities and talents that have no obvious value outside of a traditional Christian home, which God has withheld from us.

God told me I was special to Him, and I believed Him. So I never learned to care about impressing people. The Bible says He desired me (Psalm 45:11). So I pursued God and never hunted down a relationship—but how I coveted one.

God told me I was made by Him (and He makes no mistakes), and I took Him at His word. So I never learned to hide my flaws. As I studied, I knew God expected me to be wise. So I never practiced flirtation or even how to return interest without blushing.

God told me He had a plan and would faithfully guide me in it. It was all in His time, the Bible said. So I trusted Him (kind of).

And I ended up alone.

How many times I told God all that, I couldn't begin to guess. But it wasn't just a few. And my situation remained static.

Long hours were spent rehashing my childhood and life. What had gone wrong? What had I done wrong? What had my parents done wrong? I sifted through everything in detail and parsed out every possible contributor to my singleness. Here is what I came up with:

Top Ten Practical Reasons I Am Single

1. I grew up in the middle of nowhere, and Christian boys were few and far between.
2. We moved a lot, so I never got a chance to develop relationships with boys.
3. I never dated because if I knew I wasn't interested in a man as a husband, I turned down the offer . . .
4. . . . and very few Christian guys ever even asked.
5. I am a poor flirt because I never learned how.
6. I am a hard match, and I have been told I'm a bit scary (too intense).
7. I never tried to fix myself because as I evaluated myself by God's Word it seemed like I was on the right track.
8. I never tried to fix my situation because finding a husband is God's job; my job is to follow Him wherever He leads.
9. There are lots of reasons . . . but the bottom line is:
10. God (I'm pretty sure) never brought the right man.

So even though it's not what I want, that is the truth about why I am still single—and it *is* God's fault.

In the same way that it is a quarterback's fault his football team won the game, God knowingly allows us to be single. Yes, our choices influence this. But—and it has taken me fifteen years to be able to say this—at the end of the game, it is in His goodness and His sovereignty that God purposefully and graciously leads us to this life. We are single by God's design, and He will empower us to flourish and fulfill His good plans for us.

REFLECT

How did you get where you are in your relationship status? Is God surprised? If He has redeemed you against the odds, isn't He also able to bring about good using your circumstances?

PRAY

If you cannot praise God yet for your singleness, that is okay. But not being able to praise Him yet is not an excuse to not praise Him ever. Today ask Jesus to show you how to praise Him for using and working through the situation you are in (regardless of whose fault it is). And, I know, that is a hard prayer to pray.

TAKE A SINGLE STEP

Today is the day to repent of your sins (like me making marriage an idol), receive God's forgiveness, and be free to move ahead.

Confession 3

THE UNLOVED

I WAS NEARING MY LAST semester in physician assistant (PA) school and looked forward to any opportunity to leave behind the books. So I was all about it when my sister suggested a hike up the side of a huge rock, Stone Mountain. (Stone Mountain in Georgia is the East's answer to Mount Rushmore.) And a friend was coming. A friend named Carson.

A male friend named Carson, with brown hair, light eyes (not quite blue), and a scar on his cheek. He was pretty cute, in good shape, and liked the outdoors. He wasn't much of a conversational-ist, but during the hike I got him to talk.

And maybe we would have made a decent couple, except for one thing: he liked my sister.

And this is where a live audience grimaces and reflexively says, "Ohhh."

Okay, I confess: I don't really mind people looking down their noses at me and sniffing, "She just couldn't catch a man." I can live with words like that . . . as long as they aren't true. But what if they are? Maybe I am not married just because I am not woman enough to snag a man. Maybe I am defective.

As singles, we can easily look at marriage as a stamp of approval from God, the opposite sex, the world at large, and maybe even ourselves. We can equate a relationship with acceptance and success. And if we view marriage this way, it is easy to see why the opposite—that is, being single—would be a sign of rejection and evidence of failure.

The problem is, no one can just say, "Oh, marriage doesn't mean that," because some of those things are undeniably true. In some ways marriage can be a sign of approval. Someone wants to be with you, love you, support you, and receive the same from you for life. Getting a high-powered job is not like that. Graduating valedictorian is not either. And as great as it is, neither is adopting a dog.

Nope, marriage is the one time a person, any person, chooses you for life. And that speaks volumes. You are validated as worthy, lovable, attractive.

However, there are also some important lies buried in that view of marriage.

Lie 1: Marriage is God's stamp of approval.

In Regency-era author Jane Austen's time, "A single man in possession of a good fortune" may indeed "be in want of a wife,"[1] but in our culture, rich or not, to a large extent we choose whether we marry. Some choose wisely and some do not. But according to business magnate (not paradigm of virtue) Warren Buffett, who you marry is the most critical ingredient to success. It makes more difference in your day-to-day life than any other choice.[2] (Except, I would interject, trusting and following Jesus as Savior and Lord.)

Because marriage is an optional life choice, it is unwise to assume God is pleased with someone merely because they are married (or engaged) or because they are single, for that matter. This would be like looking at someone's house and extrapolating God's favor based on the color, size, or location. People have wanted to do this for thousands of years (Psalm 73), but the fact is simple: a person's life (and God's favor) is not measured by the stuff the person has, relationally or otherwise (Luke 12:15).

Lie 2: Marriage proves a person's value.

He was a single dad with two girls. She was a single mom with three boys. I know them both. The only thing they have in common (outside of being smart, wonderful people and agreeing on politics and religion) is both their spouses left them, their marriages, and their kids. But abandonment didn't change their value as individuals.

A person's value is assigned by God—not the way they look, what skills they have, or the things they have obtained in life. As soon as we start looking at marriage as this checkbox that says "Jane or John has arrived," we are deluding ourselves. Many have checked that box and then are confused when marriage doesn't yield what they want. And it won't. It can't, because if this is our expectation—that marriage will fulfill us—we are refusing to believe the truth: we are complete in Christ (Colossians 2:10).

Marriage is God's idea. Hence, it is a good thing. It provides companionship and accountability. It is a safe haven and an avenue for growth. God gave us marriage to enjoy life and expand His kingdom. But even an excellent spouse and a healthy marriage can't fill the need in our hearts for validation, because that hole is there for God.

In his book *Discovering God's Will*, Sinclair Ferguson writes, "We make the mistake of thinking that marriage will provide the ultimate satisfaction for which we all hunger. . . . Only God satisfies the hungry heart. Marriage is but one of the channels He uses to enable us to taste how deeply satisfying His thirst-quenching grace can be."[3]

Christ and His love fills our void.

"But you [insert your name here] are a chosen generation, a royal priesthood, a holy nation, His own special people, that you may proclaim the praises of Him who called you out of darkness into His marvelous light" (1 Peter 2:9).

So whether we die unloved or marry tomorrow, we have defects (that Christ is redeeming), but we are not defective.

I think Leah grasped this . . . eventually.

In the story of Rachel and Leah (Genesis 29–31), Rachel was the beautiful younger sister who captured Jacob's heart. Leah was the ugly (and, some people think, heavier) older daughter who stole her sister's lover. And while Rachel was the loved wife, Leah was the first wife. She held the position of authority in the house, just as she always had as the oldest daughter. Rachel was the one who couldn't get pregnant, while Leah had seven children, six of them sons. Leah had everything.

Everyone should pity and relate to Rachel. But Leah has always been my favorite. And as I have matured, this has grown increasingly true because Leah was the unloved one.

All human hearts yearn to be loved. Not just loved, but known and loved—as Rachel was by Jacob. We have a fear of being rejected. The deepest part of this fear is that we will be known and judged undeserving—as Leah was by Jacob.

We desire to be known so others can affirm our gifts and tell us we have value. We need others to like us, enjoy our sense of humor, and appreciate our personality. But being known also opens us up to ridicule and condescension because we can now be rejected as substandard and unworthy of love. And that was where Leah found herself.

She was known by her husband, and he considered her inferior. She ran a large household. She bore six heirs for the family name. She did everything expected of her, and she did it masterfully. Even so, she never captured the one thing she yearned for: her husband's affection and approval.

But when Leah named her fourth son, she called him Judah, saying, "Now I will praise the LORD" (Genesis 29:35). This was the first time, in naming four sons, she didn't mention her husband.

Just because a diamond mine is undiscovered doesn't change its value. Just because others do not approve of you doesn't mean you are unloved.

Diamonds are always valuable. And we are always loved.

Partway through her loveless marriage—one in which she actually had to purchase Jacob's companionship (Genesis 30:15)—Leah seemed to have grasped the truth: God fully knew her. He loved her, and He said she had purpose and worth. The Bible says God proved His love to her by opening her womb, thereby giving her a secure future (Genesis 29:31).

God has done the same for us.

> Christ has proven His love to you by providing Himself as the only possible sacrifice to rescue you from sin, death, and yourself.

His love for us is not proven by a godly marriage. It is not proven by seven healthy children. Our value is not even proven by having a thriving ministry.

Christ has proven His love to you by providing Himself as the only possible sacrifice to rescue you from sin, death, and yourself. When we believe this, Jesus becomes our Savior and Lord. The Holy Spirit indwells us. The Father adopts us as His daughters. He proves His love by giving us access to heaven in prayer (Ephesians 2:18) and assurance of an eternal future which starts now by knowing God (John 17:3).

We are single, but we are God's—known, loved, and valued by Him. We don't need to pursue a human relationship to find these things. They are already true of us.

REFLECT

God knows, loves, and values you. How should this impact how you view yourself and how you view others?

PRAY

Acknowledge God's perfect understanding of you, your hurts, and your desires. Accept God's unconditional love. And rejoice in your value to Him right now, as you are.

TAKE A SINGLE STEP

Draw a flower below. On each petal, write something God says you are. (Ephesians 1–2 is a great place to look if you are stumped.)

Confession 4

THE POWERHOUSE AWARDS

YOU HAVE KNOWN WOMEN LIKE her, I'm sure. Everyone knew she wanted to get married, but no one in our small group thought she was desperate enough to marry a man who

1. wasn't a Christian;
2. had no way of supporting her (or the baby on the way); and
3. possessed the personality of a wet dishrag.

Turns out we were wrong.

A few years ago, I was running through the marriages of my siblings, friends, and acquaintances and considering: How many of these marriages made both partners better servants of God and His kingdom?

I was forced to the sad conclusion that it was rare for marriage to improve both individuals' spiritual well-being. In fact, even among my Christian friends, too many marriages were obviously the result of impatience and lust rather than submission to the will of God. Because, really, who wants to wait? The Bible tells us we are self-serving by nature, and our choices, even life-changing ones, too often reflect that self-absorption.

That's one way you can tell the Bible is true: it never sugarcoats anything. Situations, people, and couples are recorded in sordid detail. In fact, there are a lot more messed-up couples in the Bible than powerhouse couples.

You've got Abraham and Sarah, who brought in a surrogate mother to give them a son . . . yup, that worked not so well.

Then you've got Rebekah, who was over there tricking Isaac into blessing her favorite son. Healthy marriage? I think not.

Then there's Jacob and Leah . . . and Rachel . . . and Bilhah . . . and Zilpah and that whole debacle.

David was married to an unbelievable number of women, but his son Solomon blew everyone out of the water with his harem. (If someone could have multiple harems, it would be him.)

Hosea was married to a prostitute. Job's wife was struggling in faith. Oh yeah, can't forget Ananias and Sapphira. (At least they were greedy and deceptive together.)

And we could keep going.

But counting powerhouse couples in Scripture is easy. Noah and his wife probably make the list, though this is hard to prove due to lack of information about her. Abraham and Sarah are the only couple mentioned in the Hall of Faith (Hebrews 11), so even though I would have written them off, God clearly didn't—which is a good lesson in and of itself. Even a powerhouse couple will make mistakes, but with God they can recover from them and be restored.

The marriage of Ruth and Boaz must be on any list of Spirit-led, God-filled marriages. After all, no other marriage gets an entire book dedicated to its love story—except the one between God and us. The Bible also specifically points out the godliness of both Zacharias and Elizabeth, so they make the cut. But Joseph and Mary are probably the most obvious couple for such a list, followed closely by Priscilla and Aquila, Paul's friends and fellow workers.

I may have missed some but that's all I found: six. Six couples in 1,500 pages of biblical narrative.

To be fair, we simply don't know enough about the wives of many men mentioned in the Bible to officially label them powerhouse couples, which is encouraging. Since we don't know otherwise, maybe the Peters, Josephs (Old Testament), Isaiahs, Ezekiels, and Jameses were powerhouse couples too. And if they were, our odds of becoming part of a powerhouse couple are mathematically improving. There are some almost-powerhouse couples in the Scriptures. Adam and Eve win the Should-Have-Been Award. But the almost-awesome marriage I am thinking of seems closer to full-powerhouse status.

Ready for some clues?

- This *almost* powerhouse was already married.
- He was a king (of Israel), and she was a prophetess.
- He was decisive, and she was too.
- He was crafty and full of faith, and she was intelligent and wise.

Know who it is? Well, if not, this one will give it away: he was a man after God's own heart, and she was the widow of Nabal. David was a shepherd-turned-warrior king, and Abigail was a silver-tongued negotiator. What a pair.

My theory is that Abigail was the woman God had picked for David, but he smudgied it. Here's the story (or you can read the whole thing in 1 Samuel 25).

David and his men were hiding out in the hills, safe from Saul and safeguarding the flocks of a man name Nabal. After months of protecting Nabal's sheep and servants, David sent a few men to Nabal's large estate for a reward. A greedy, evil man, Nabal refused to give them anything except ridicule and insults. And David was angry—angry enough to want to kill Nabal and every man in his house.

A small army marched down on Nabal's domain to destroy it. But the servants who'd heard Nabal's pompous rebuff of David scurried to Abigail and begged her to arbitrate. Abigail, immediately discerning their peril, ordered the servants to load up a passel of donkeys with bread, wine, dressed sheep, fruit, and grain, and then she left to meet David herself. In a display of skilled diplomacy, Abigail reminded David of his accountability to God and reiterated God's promises to him. Doing so saved her household and her husband.

The next morning when Abigail told him the news, Nabal's "heart died within him" (1 Samuel 25:37), and within ten days he died. David then proposed to Abigail, who became one of his wives.

And that was the problem. David was already married.

The Scriptures portray Abigail as beautiful, intelligent, and insightful into the ways and plans of God. Based on how accurately Abigail foretells David's future, many believe she was one of the few biblical prophetesses. So if any woman was ready to become half of a powerhouse couple, Abigail was. But the potential powerhouse marriage couldn't happen because of David's mistakes in love.

Mistakes in love matter.

Trial and error works in many things. But in love, trial and error is like carving an ice sculpture: each try diminishes the potential for the future.

Looking in on couples like David and Abigail (and many others) from afar, we often see more disastrous and foolish marriages than powerhouse matches. Witnessing the propensity of the human race to smudgie it should help us temper our vigor to intervene on our behalf and rein in the temptation to patch together a quick fix for our singleness by getting married.

There's more to marriage than simply snaring a partner. Like a surfer waiting for the best wave possible, you and I are holding out for a marriage worth waiting for—a Christian powerhouse. Two doctors get married—a medical powerhouse. Two athletes—a sports powerhouse. Two Christians who get married are designed to be a spiritual powerhouse.

One often feels like an orphan, while a couple is the obvious foundation for a home and a family. As such it is little wonder we pursue this human relationship so hard and often to our detriment. The challenge is to recognize the beautiful potential within marriage and respect it enough to wait. God has not left us as orphans (John 14:18), nor kept us as servants. Married or not, He has called us friends (John 15:15).

So for now, in that grace, we hold out as single powerhouses. For ourselves. For our future husbands. For the children God might grant us. But most importantly, for our Savior. We strive to have the greatest impact for His kingdom, knowing in our service to God we find our greatest joy and fulfillment. For our unborn children, we realize having a mother who is in love with and in open fellowship with Jesus Christ is the best gift we can give. For our one-day husbands, we acknowledge becoming a woman after God's own heart is more important for his pleasure and success than rushing into a relationship.

May the kingdom of God advance to the greatest possible degree first while we remain a single powerhouse for God and then, if He wills, when we marry into a spiritual powerhouse for Him. The Scriptures demonstrate convincingly that this is only possible with and for God. Because unless the Lord builds a house, they labor in vain to build it, and unless He guards a city, the watchman stays awake for no reason (Psalm 127:1).

But with God, anything is possible (Matthew 19:26). So the opportunity of a spiritual powerhouse marriage may come, and if it comes, we should pursue it as God's best and for Christ's kingdom. Until then, Lord, help Your powerhouse singles to focus and fulfill Your calling.

—— REFLECT ——

How does focusing on God and His service prepare you to be part of a possible future powerhouse couple while you fulfill God's will today?

—— PRAY ——

Pray God's blessings on the couples you know. Ask God to make them powerhouse couples for His kingdom.

—— TAKE A SINGLE STEP ——

Do one thing today you know God is asking you to do. How does this prepare you to become half of a powerhouse couple?

Confession 5

DEAR GOD, SIGN THIS

IF YOU WENT TO SUMMER camp as a kid, you will appreciate this. Today I got to hike around the camp where I went to Survival as a teenager. (Survival was a summer camp that focused on wilderness and spiritual survival.) As I walked the old paths, I visited the boys' side of camp (gasp), which, disappointingly, looked like the girls' side. I found the cabin where the bear played with my shoes, and I was struck by this thought: if you had marched up to me back then and told me, "God wants you to have a medical career and stay single at least until your midthirties," I would have broken down in tears. I would have been completely inconsolable, because as a teen at camp, my life plan looked like this:

Dear God,
Here is my life plan:
I want to get married by age 21.
I want to be a mother.
I want to have 12 children.
I want to homeschool.

I am open to international ministry. (Can creature comforts be provided?)

I decline to go to college, so I can be ready for a fantastic marriage.

Please initial each line, date, and then sign at the bottom.

Love,
Alisha

Over fifteen-plus years, God has made a lot of changes to my life plan:

Dear God,

Here is my life plan:

I want to get married by age ~~21, 24, 27,~~ 31?

I want to be a mother, ~~doctor, mother, mother and doctor, doctor,~~ and a medical professional.

I want to have ~~12, 9, 6~~ children.

I want to homeschool.

I am open to international ministry. (Can creature comforts be provided?)

~~I decline to go to college.~~

Fine, I will go to college until I get married.

I want to go to medical school.

Okay, You win—I guess I will go to physician assistant (PA) school.

And be a PA until . . . You intervene? (Feel free to strike this one out.)

Love,
Alisha

If you had sprung all those changes on me at once, I would have been so distraught at the snapshot of my future life that I think it's likely I would have straight up quit. What is truly ironic is that this revelation is exactly what I wanted from God. I wanted Him to lay out a complete life plan (preferably in writing) from now until death. I had this prayer on repeat from ages twelve to twenty-five.

And I remember the moment distinctly when I thought God was going to answer my prayer.

"Do you want to know what God's will is for your life?"

My wide eyes sparkled. *Yes! Yes!* I silently rejoiced and leaned forward, twitching in excitement. I had been looking for this for years. I held my breath as the speaker continued.

"If you want to know God's will, find a concordance and locate every place the Bible says this is God's will. And then do it."

I breathed again and didn't write down anything. That was his secret? Who doesn't know what God wants for *everyone*? I needed to know exactly what He wanted for me. Should I go to college? If so, where? What should my major be? How could I ensure the best possible life for myself?

I understood the words of the secret immediately, but I didn't understand the truth of it. The truth took more than a decade to grasp, but this is it: all Christ-followers live by faith, obeying one step at a time. Not even the heroes of faith were handed a road map to make their perfect life happen.

But as a teen, that is what I wanted. So I waited and waited and waited some more. I was convinced God's plan would be revealed to me en masse. Maybe after I graduated . . . or had a job . . . or did this or that . . . Surely it was just around the next corner.

And I found out if you—like me—hold out for that elusive road map, you will end up wandering through life lukewarm, engaging half-heartedly and ineffectively because "it" could be coming and you have to be ready. Your prayers become dry, repeat demands for direction. Instead of praising God, it becomes easy to constantly complain that you are still waiting. And instead of worshipping the Lord through joyous, abundant service, you postpone living while waiting for life to start.

Years later I can finally admit: I couldn't handle the truth. If God had given in to my whining—to get everything, all at once—I would have rebelled and done things my way. But praise God, He only tells us what we need to know for the day. Because God didn't answer my (oft-repeated) prayer and allowed me to remain clueless about the future, He provided me the opportunity to be happy, obedient, and purposeful, like God's servants are supposed to be. But even though I went through the Christian motions, I couldn't see my singleness as an opportunity, because my feelings didn't match what I knew, and what I knew didn't match what I wanted.

Still, God's approach was spot-on. Couldn't see that one coming, could you? (I promise at nineteen, I might have said I could, but I couldn't.)

One choice, one word, one action at a time—that's all we have to do, and it's all we can do. I can't live all of Alisha's life in one fell swoop. Even super-Christians can't do that. They have to be obedient one step at a time too. And I must confess, I am grateful not to be a lot of biblical characters. Like Noah, who put up with years of public ridicule; or Ruth, a destitute Gentile widow who had to propose to an older man; or especially Isaiah, who walked around naked. John the Baptist. David. Elijah. Abraham. Peter. Jeremiah. People in the Bible did dangerous, crazy, unthinkable, impossible things to please God. He asked and enabled, and they obeyed with "Yes, Lord."

God isn't likely to ask us to dig through a wall or lie on the same side for weeks or go and restore someone's vision. But He has the right to—He is God, after all.

But God is not asking us to do what they did. We often wonder,

Would I leave my family and wander in the desert for God? Would I dance for God in the streets? And though those are good thoughts to ponder, the question that really matters is, *Will I obey God today?*

There is no way to tell what God's ask will be, what it will require, how long it will take, or where it will take us. Obedience is a land of few guarantees and much uncertainty. But to conquer that land is our calling, our responsibility, and our privilege. Will you go? Before you say yes, prepare yourself for a shock: it's going to cost your life (Matthew 10:39) and your goals for life (Mark 8:35). Yes, those are two different things. One is the denial of self, and one is the acceptance of God's will in place of our own. It took me years to learn "if anyone desires to come after Me, let him deny himself, and take up his cross, and follow Me" (Matthew 16:24).

🔖

As a kid, the best place to be on a sticky, summer day was Sunset Beach. It wasn't just the sun, sand, and surf; it was the snack shop! And New York State paid five cents per aluminum can, which were never in short supply. That translated into candy—Swedish Fish in particular. I turned in my cans and got sweets in return.

It was a great lesson in money management, economics, and diligence. It was not a great lesson about how God's economy works. Even though I subconsciously thought so for decades, God's economy is not a transaction. Good works, obedience, and sacrifices do not translate into coupons for getting what we want in life.

In high school, I sacrificially told God, "I will do whatever you want." This was code for, "I will forgo college to raise a family"— which is what *I* wanted.

When that did not happen, I changed tactics and offered God my whole life in medical service as a doctor. I thought maybe if I lavishly offered God something I didn't think He wanted, I could make Him come to His senses and give in to my goals. More than anything, I wanted to get married and have a family. And I confess: somewhere deep inside I thought I could trick God into giving me what I wanted. Of course, I would never have said this is what I was doing, because I didn't know it myself. But this I do know: my bartering did not work.

God shut the door to medical school twice, and in defeat I went to physician assistant school. I was deflated and seriously doubting God's goodness, because even though I had done everything right to pay for a great husband, marriage, and children, He hadn't given them to me.

But now that I was free from the drudgery of medical school, residency, and fellowship, I sped through my master's degree. I was secretly hoping this was the way to achieve my end point—namely, a family of my own. But it wasn't, and I found myself in clinical practice for far longer than I had anticipated. Confused and discouraged, a battle raged in my heart and mind. And so when my obedience (inevitably) did not result in what I most desired (yes, even more than God), I was angry because in that secret part of me, I felt God had cheated me. I had paid the price and didn't get what I paid for. As these wrong lines of reasoning hit the cold hard facts of life, and they led into a smoldering bitterness against God.

Yes, I still obeyed, but I obeyed many years with great inner turmoil. I surrendered to God's will and hand so often, I can't even pick out a discrete memory of doing it. God had control of my thoughts, attitudes, and actions—but not my motives.

My strategy was to obey God but to have my obedience lead to my destination—marriage. I was planning to get what I wanted by doing life God's way. So I was following His instructions, and I can provide convincing evidence I was committed to doing so. But when my obedience did not lead where I thought it should, I was emotionally devastated because I thought that was the deal.

This idea is akin to a kid moving from the attitude of "I eat my veggies because Mom says they are good for me . . . but I want them to taste like brownies" to "I eat my veggies because they are good for me like Mom says."

To give God control is simply to align your thinking with reality.

In the first, we eat our broccoli with the purpose of it tasting like brownies. We all know how well that works. No matter how good your imagination, broccoli (or your least favorite veggie) will never taste like brownies, just like obeying God will never yield exclusively what you want. In the second scenario, we have accepted the truth: vegetables are good for us even if they never taste like brownies. And this is the point from which all Christians are called to operate.

To give God control is simply to align your thinking with reality. He is, always has been, and always will be in control. You are not, which is good. And once you realize this, God's presence is able to fill your life with joy and security as you rest in God's strength to intervene and direct.

But it is possible to do all this and still have a goal for your obedience that does not match God's. Therefore, the why you do things, the why you say things, and the why you pray things all must be fundamentally altered to match God's heart and plan for you. You must abandon your goals before God's throne and let Him decide when and if those goals will be fulfilled in your life.

That is where I found myself when I finally realized obeying God wasn't getting me what I wanted—because godly obedience is not a contract. Remember Job? Obeying God did not work for him . . . not by a long shot.

If we have trusted in Jesus as our Savior, we are God's daughters, and with or without our buy-in, God is working in our lives to accomplish the best goals possible: His goals. There is no long con with God. There is no way to manipulate Him into giving us the blessings we want. Obedience is not the purchase price for marriage or children or anything else in life. Rather, His goals must be the motivation for our ambitions, and His ways must become ours. And frankly, we want that . . . because we make mistakes, but how many mistakes does God make?

When God has control and our motives match His, obedience is a joy, and the peace that passes all understanding guards our hearts and minds (Philippians 4:6–7). God has never done us wrong and never will. Whether we marry or not, His plan is what we want for our lives.

Dear God,
I want to please You, and to that end I will obey You. I will follow You. I will serve You. Even if I never get what I think I want, I know You will give what is truly good because You promise You withhold no good thing (Psalm 84:11), and You are the One who never lies (Titus 1:2).

Help me trust You, Father, as You mold my heart to want what You want. Amen.

REFLECT

Why do you fear allowing God to fully direct your life?

PRAY

Take time in prayer to worship God for who He is, and review His character qualities, remembering how they ensure you abundant life, now and forever.

—— TAKE A SINGLE STEP ——

Write a letter (like the one above) to God, and surrender your life, life plans, and life goals to Him. Set an alarm on your phone for the next week (or longer) to remind yourself: "I am God's. I am going where He wants, when He wants, how He wants, to achieve whatever He wants."

Confession 6

A WONDERFUL MYSTERY

How DOES IT FEEL WHEN you stumble upon a mystery? Mysteries intrigue some of us, and they irritate others. But spiritual mysteries, like godliness, have the potential to raise our eyes to our Creator in worship and in awe.

I Feel Selfish

Don't tell anyone, but white elephant gift exchanges are one of my least favorite Christmas traditions. Yes, a few people end up insanely pleased with their gifts. But most of us end up with creepy Santa Claus mugs we won't use.

The reason we even have white elephant gift exchanges is because in history, white elephants were revered. But they were too special to do any work. So being given a white elephant was an honor . . . that came with the burden of feeding this multiton animal that couldn't be used for anything.

God's gifts are not like this. He isn't haphazardly assigning people skills or opportunities or life circumstances, or giving people gifts that they can't use. He purposefully gives us gifts we are able to use.

He has given gifts to everyone:

For I wish that all men were even as I myself. But each one has his own gift from God, one in this manner and another in that. (1 Corinthians 7:7)

Our Savior's gifts are not a burden:

For My yoke is easy and My burden is light. (Matthew 11:30)

God's gifts are useful:

As each one has received a gift, minister it to one another, as good stewards of the manifold grace of God. (1 Peter 4:10)

And that is something you and I need to be reminded of when we look at our friends, family members, or random women at the post office and think, *She is doing something that matters.* I have certainly thought this. My sister-in-law, for example, is a military wife whose husband gets back soon from a six-month deployment. They have three little ones under the age of six (and her plan is to make that four in the near future). She homeschools the oldest and takes the middle one to therapy five times a week. She bakes for their church, neighbors, and friends. She works in the church nursery and still manages to find time to keep up with fellow moms.

I don't do any of those things.

I generally do what I please. I sleep eight hours or more without interruption, unless my dog happens to bark in her sleep. My time is largely my own. And in comparison (which I know is unwise, 2 Corinthians 10:12), I feel selfish. There is no husband to make sack lunches for or little noses to wipe or family activities to attend. And this realization makes me stomp my feet. "God, I have such a self-centered life! Can't I have her gifts?" (And here all the moms say in stereo, "Are you crazy?!" And the answer is, "Probably.")

But the real question is, How will we use our gifts?

I can pretend singleness is not my gift (even though it clearly is right now because I am single). I can pray to have my sister-in-law's gifts, and believe me, I have done that plenty. I can waste time envying her, which I have also done. I can work to have her gifts—and even feel guilty about not having her life mission. But not one of these is being a good steward of God's grace to me as His single.

Or I can accept the truth, which is that at this moment, singleness is God's gift to me. I can pray for direction on how to best use my time and my opportunities in my singleness, no matter how long it lasts. I can choose to thank God for my gifts and glorify Him by working hard with the gifts I have been given. And all of these demonstrate wise stewardship of God's grace.

Besides, everyone knows the best attitude to take to a white elephant gift exchange is, *Who can I pawn off this gift on?* In all of the best ways of course! Applied to singleness, we might say the God-honoring attitude is, *Who can I disciple and encourage with this gift?*

I Feel Small

Ever wonder if what you do matters? If the hard choices you make will change anything? I think at some point all of us do. That's what I mean when I say I feel small—as if my contributions to God's kingdom couldn't possibly make a difference. *It's just leading our kids' club or teaching Sunday school or praying with the prayer team*, we might think. How far can our daily acts of service really reach? Well, twenty feet doesn't seem that far, until you are peering off a cliff into the water and you hear, "Jump! Jump!"

Standing there, looking down, I suddenly understood why the application for the navy specifically asked if I would be able to launch myself off a platform twelve feet into the water. I had checked yes without a second thought. Now I wasn't too sure.

I stood at the tip of the precipice for what seemed like an hour.

And it may not have been a full sixty minutes, but it was long enough for a boat of drunken frat boys to drift by and yell various suggestive things at me. That was unnerving. I backed away from the drop-off, but I still wanted to jump. So I devised a plan. The next time I came to the edge, I didn't look down. I looked straight out and jumped. My first thought was, *I am going to die.*

Then I hit the water, and my next thought was, *I'm alive!* I came up grinning. As I swam to shore, I stared up the cliff, and from this perspective, I felt tiny (but incredibly grateful to be alive).

Married or single, if we feel small, it's because we are. And if we don't feel small, it's because we are out of touch with reality. It's so easy to translate that small feeling into the conclusion that our efforts to serve God can't possibly be making an impact. But truly understanding our role in God's kingdom as a small one is both accurate and comforting. God is the one responsible for building His church. In His grace, God is using small people to reach out and make eternal progress.

> ## Life is an epic adventure with innumerable story lines the Storyteller is weaving together toward a grand conclusion.

Life isn't a fairy tale that revolves around us as individuals. Life is an epic adventure with innumerable story lines the Storyteller is weaving together toward a grand conclusion. He is taking all the small people and small ministries and crafting a masterful story line. A correct perspective of ourselves is not meant to be a discouragement (though it will be if we focus on it); it is meant to be a neon sign directing us to focus on the Storyteller and His plans.

As we focus on God, we are able to view ourselves for what we are, characters in His story. As His characters, we gain purpose. The Storyteller says we have a part to play in His tale—right now.

God isn't tapping His watch, saying, "Hurry up and get married so I can use you."

Not at all. God is coaxing, "Come on! Jump! I've got plans for you, but you have to jump!"

That means we have to stop staring at how big the cliff is. We have to block out the voices of the drunken frat boys, because regardless of what they are saying, they aren't telling us what we need to hear. And we need to look straight ahead at whatever God is calling us to do—and jump!

You and I are single and feel small. That means nothing can hold us back from God's will except us.

Therefore, we do not grow weary in doing good—or allow ourselves to be fooled into believing small means expendable. Instead, we can be confident that we will see the fruit of our labors as long as we don't give up (Galatians 6:9).

I Feel Insecure

Have you ever envied a princess locked in a tower? I have. Her life is very secure and straightforward. It's simple. She is locked in a tower and will remain so until her Prince Charming rescues her. They shall then be wed and live happily ever after. Amen . . . er, the end.

A Christian spinster's life is not like that. Her life is open ended and subject to change, and more than a little security challenged. If God said go to Africa—she could. If God said work in politics—she could. If God said quit your job and run a nonprofit—she could.

See, a princess always knows for sure she hasn't missed Prince Charming, because she is still in the tower. But a Christian spinster has probably considered this question carefully multiple times and is 96.7 percent confident she hasn't missed him (+/- 2.6 percent).

Our princess knows exactly what to do with her life: wait for Prince Charming (and hopefully, he comes before she is wrinkled and gray). And truthfully, many a Christian spinster would like to do this. But it gets boring. And, most importantly, she's pretty sure it doesn't please God.

The hardest thing a towered princess has to answer is the ageless question: If she can escape her tower without the prince, should she? Or would this wreck her chance to be with Prince Charming? Which only leads her to begin wondering how easy it might be to get in and out of the tower. If she can get out, anyone can get in. And if anyone can get in, who's to say it will be Prince Charming who will show up. It's a conundrum.

But a Christian spinster has a harder question to answer: Where does security come from?

If it comes from towers, she could just buy one.

If it comes from princes, she could go find one.

If it comes from money, she could devote herself to securing a fortune.

But it doesn't.

Security, and the desire for it, comes from God, with whom we dwell forever.

> Surely goodness and mercy shall follow me
> All the days of my life;
> And I will dwell in the house of the LORD
> Forever. (Psalm 23:6)

The princess in a tower can just stay in her castle—forever bored, useless, and secure.

But if a Christian spinster desires security, she must actively receive God's truth and rule over her thoughts (2 Corinthians 10:3–6).

She has to learn the truth and banish thoughts that exalt themselves against God to experience the security He offers her. She must infuse into her heart and mind the Word of Christ and submit her every thought to Him. Then God may do as He has always desired and satisfy her craving for true security with the reality of His presence. Then she will never be bored or useless (2 Peter 1:5–8).

For eye has not seen, ear has not heard, and man's heart cannot even imagine the good things God has prepared for those who love Him (1 Corinthians 2:9).

Being single makes me feel *selfish* like a Siamese cat, *small* like a guppy fish, and *insecure* like a flying squirrel. And the composite of those three animals is not compatible with life, so no wonder I have issues. But praise God He gave Paul an answer for these feelings when Paul said, "Look, who cares what men say or think? I don't even judge myself. God is my judge. He will uncover all things—even things I wish He wouldn't—and everything worthy of praise He will reward" (1 Corinthians 4:3–5, author's paraphrase).

We may be selfish, but God is the perfect gift-giver, and He is using us.

We are small, but God is great, and He is using us.

We might feel insecure, but God is invincible, and He is using us.

This is a wonderful mystery.

REFLECT

What keeps you from seeing your singleness as a gift?

PRAY

Ask God for His perspective on your life. Ask Him to reveal how He's using you.

TAKE A SINGLE STEP

Today is the day to jump in and receive God's gifts.

If you struggle with feeling selfish, what gifts has God given you and how are you using them sacrificially? Then jump into service.

If you struggle with feeling small, what is God asking you to do today? Is God great enough to accomplish that through you? Then jump into His adventure.

If you struggle with feeling insecure, what lies are you telling yourself about security? What is the truth about God's invincibility? Then jump into His arms.

Confession 7

THE RING

No, NOT *THAT* RING, YOU LotR (Lord of the Rings) fanatics—the actual ring. The ring that lives on one's left fourth finger. And I'll own up: I have tried basically every ring I own on that finger (just to see how it looks).

Did you know modern bridal fantasies demand a groom spend one to three months' salary on an engagement ring? *Three months*.

Why? Because our men want to make us happy. That sounds amazingly romantic until real life jumps back in the driver's seat. The utility company won't take a picture of your ring in exchange for leaving the lights on. And you may actually want to go on a honeymoon—not just look at a lump of expensive carbon on your finger. Rings are small, and they can easily disappear in the manicured grounds of your first apartment complex. True story.

But practicality notwithstanding, a ring on that finger tells the world "I am chosen." I have even thought of wearing one just so men would leave me alone. (After being hit on three times in a week in the emergency department, extrapolate the clientele . . . You get the picture.) Because having no ring tells the world "I am available."

Anyone can buy a ring. Anyone can wear a ring. My grandmother had her class ring made for her ring finger, which was ridiculous because she had four men who wanted to marry her. She kept all their pictures too, even after being married for more than forty years, having three children, burying a husband, greeting five grandchildren and one great grandson. Why?

Because each of those men wanted to "put a ring on it," and that ring means: someone loves me. And everyone likes to know they are valued and have evidence of it on days when they don't feel like it.

It took years before I realized that God has put a ring on it. And it cost Him a lot more than three months' salary. We were engaged after Jesus gave His life as the bride-price to purchase our freedom from sin, and we accepted that sacrifice as the only way for us to have a relationship with God now and in heaven. As proof of our covenantal relationship, His Spirit came and indwelt us (Acts 1:4–5). His daily presence in our lives is the ring—the promise we will indeed be married.

I regretfully confess I have spent far less time contemplating that wedding and that Groom and much more time contemplating my mythical earthly wedding and mortal groom. I know this because I still have my lists, covering everything wedding, bride, and, of course, groom. If you have your own lists, you'll understand.

Alisha's Top Ten List for Eligible Men
(From nearly two decades ago! Yikes.)

1. Tall
2. Blond
3. Blue eyes
4. Athletic
5. Smart
6. Adventurous
7. From the country
8. Good job

9. Loves Jesus
10. ?????

Anne Shirley's (*Anne of Green Gables*) perfect man was consistently tall, dark, and handsome—a man who could be wicked and wouldn't.

Alisha's perfect man was never well described, even in my mind, because my type kept changing. So my lists kept changing. Blond hair or black hair? As long as he looked nice under it, what difference did it make? Same with eyes, so 2 and 3 quickly fell off the list. As a young woman, I thought "adventurous" defined the image of a bad boy, which appealed to me. But with time, this quality seemed less and less an asset and more and more a warning sign, so 6 became negotiable.

The only thing that seemed to remain constant for very long was 1 (tall), preferably five foot eleven or up. And now, as I have gotten older and (hopefully) wiser, even the tall part of my type has been pushed off to the wayside as 9 began to climb the ranks and eventually topped the list.

I found myself drawn more and more to men who were filled with the Holy Spirit and were serving God with all they had. Men who were humbly living out their love for God and others became attractive regardless of how they physically appeared. As I matured, I noticed joyful, self-controlled men who were glorifying God. Those who delighted in the Word of God and who were courageously countercultural as a result now drew my interest—even if they were short.

Alisha's Modified Top Ten List
(From about ten years ago.)

1. Loves God
2. Seeks God
3. Actively serves God

4. Ready to lead
5. Filled with the Holy Spirit
6. Humble
7. Courageous
8. Joyful
9. Kind
10. Lives in full obedience to God

Being filled with the Holy Spirit . . . where had I heard that before? Humble, courageous, joyful, and kind, living fully in obedience to God? Didn't I know Someone like that? Those things all seemed strangely familiar. But I made lists for years without realizing the truth.

I already knew this Man. He already knew me. And we are already engaged.

His name is Jesus. No man can check off those boxes with impunity, but Jesus can and already has. No human can fulfill those kinds of expectations in marriage—he will surely fail. But Jesus can more than fulfill those. His life was perfect, so He actually demonstrates to me what my expectations of a Savior should be. Through His Holy Spirit, He and I can live in constant fellowship. Jesus is fully prepared to lead me and love me in this marriage.

Our human marriages may or may not happen. Children might or might not be in our future. And yet Jesus was and is and will be everything on our perfect-man lists at all times and in all places. Married or single, if we are living with Christ as Savior and Lord, He is our Husband.

God greatly desires to have a relationship with each one of us as individuals, and this is reflected in us. John and Stasi Eldredge, founders of Wild at Heart, point out in *Captivating* that "the vast desire and capacity a woman has for intimate relationships tells us of God's vast desire and capacity for intimate relationships."[1]

However, we are born with a problem that makes intimacy with God impossible: sin. Our wrong actions, words, thoughts, and attitudes separate each of us from a perfect God. And yet God's love for you and me is so deep that Jesus, God the Son, who knew no sin, became sin for us that we might be reunited in relationship with God forever (2 Corinthians 5:21).

When we believe this, we no longer have to serve sin. Instead we serve God. We no longer have to love ourselves first. Instead we love God first. Through Jesus we have peace with God in this life and throughout eternity (Romans 5:1–2). And we know we are spoken for as the bride of Christ.

If you haven't begun a relationship with Jesus, today is the day. He has already spoken for you, but you must accept His proposal. Talk to God and ask Jesus for forgiveness of your sins and commit to follow Him wherever He leads (Matthew 4:19). Once you begin a relationship with Jesus, every minute of every day you are the object of a devoted love, as a bridegroom loves his chosen. Psalm 45 is a bridal psalm, a love song between the Messiah and His bride—us. Seventeen verses give voice to unbridled joy, exulting in the majesty of the Bridegroom and the glories of the bride (verses 1 and 13).

Listen closely!

He is better.

Better than our father's house and wherever we've come from.

So much better than our wildest dreams for the future (verse 10).

Our glory shall no longer be with our fathers or the heritage they have left us. Instead, we will take pleasure in our sons—those who carry the legacy of our faith to unimagined heights. No longer shall our hope be in the past, but in the future that Christ is going to produce using us (verse 16).

Our Groom is handsome, kindly spoken, and blessed of God (verse 2). We are beautiful and desirable. God Himself desires our beauty (verse 11). And why not? It is by His hand and for His pleasure. Our

Husband's sword is fearsome in skill, triumphant in glory, and arrayed in victory (verse 3). We are robed in gold and rich colors (verse 13)—a virgin bride saved for the enjoyment of our King (verse 14).

Wondrous in strength, our Bridegroom is unmatched in truth, humility, and righteousness (verse 4). He is a man of war, renowned in justice (verse 5), loving what is right and hating all evil (verse 7). He is the one who exalts us so people honor us and seek our favor (verse 12). He is ours. He is adorned for us and anticipates taking us as His bride (verse 8). He will rule throughout eternity in righteousness, untainted (verse 6), and our joy will last forever (verse 17).

Who would refuse that marriage? Not me.

REFLECT

You are engaged to the creator of the universe and lover of your soul.

PRAY

Thank God for His Spirit, as your promise of an eternal relationship with Him.

TAKE A SINGLE STEP

Read through Psalm 45 and talk about it with your Groom.

Confession 8

DREAMS

REMEMBER JANE? LAST TIME WE saw her, our young horse was learning about unicorns. But today . . .

Jane's nose twitched. "Yum—honeysuckle." She sighed aloud, waking herself up from a wonderful dream. She stretched.

"Hey, Jane!" her friends Clove and Clive called. "Today's the day!"

"Today!" Jane nearly shouted, before calming herself. "Today," she repeated. Today the rancher was going to move his herd to the valley ranch.

Clive, one of the young stallions, peered at Jane. "You know, that bump between your eyes is getting worse."

Jane groaned and closed her eyes. She was aware.

"Yeah, it actually looks pointy and . . ." Clive's ears twitched as he trailed off.

Clove stuck a eye close to Jane's forehead. "*And pink!* Did you know it had turned pink?!"

"Keep it down!" Jane flushed and tried to ignore the stares. She had suspected it for a while, but she hadn't wanted to consider the possibility. She just couldn't be a . . . a . . . a unicorn! Could she?

"Maybe you should . . . should . . ." Clive looked uncomfortable.

"Do something about that," Clove filled in with a shrug.

Jane nodded and waited until they were gone to let her tears slip into the grass, where they could do some good. Today was ruined, along with every other today coming.

"What about my dreams?" she whispered to no one.

Some people don't dream. Others dream but come morning can't remember a blessed thing. But some people dream and remember their dreams in crazy detail.

Me? I am a dreamer.

In my dreams, I fly.

I fight.

I fall.

I've even died.

And more than once, I have dreamed of my husband. I have even dreamed of our wedding. Multiple times I have dreamed of having children. It's a bit like dreaming of a loved one who has died, which I have also done. You wake up with this deep ache inside that hangs on much longer than vivid memory of the dream itself.

Last night I dreamed of my son. I held him in my lap, and we had a serious conversation. He smiled up at me from under his *straight* red hair. (My hair is curly, so I can't explain the straight part.) Of course, he also had see-through teeth, which was a humorous reprieve from the characteristic ache in my chest.

But what am I supposed to do with that? What is there to do with these ingrained desires that permeate even our subconscious?

These dreams pop up out of nowhere—like my dream of my five *blond* children misbehaving at Awana, a children's ministry. I have no idea what triggered this. These adventures in my subconscious remind me pointedly, even if I haven't thought about my singleness or lack of children today or this week or even this month, that longing is still there, unchanged, unsatisfied. And as I grow older, it is more and more likely to remain indefinitely.

Can I sound unspiritual for just a minute? Jesus is always enough, but He doesn't always take away these longings. They are still there, and they sometimes hurt—to the point where I prayed every night for over a year straight for God to fix it.

Kind of like somebody in one of Jesus's parables.

Our unnamed heroine was alone. Her husband was dead. And Scripture says nothing about children. Seeing her plight, a powerful enemy seized the opportunity to cheat her out of anything she had left. There was only one man who could help her: the judge.

Everyone knew this judge was harsh and unfeeling, moved by neither the pleas of men nor the laws of God. But he was her only hope. She wrote letters, sent messengers, and tracked him to his office and his home.

"Get justice for me!" was her repeated cry. And the uncaring judge, who was deaf to man and indifferent toward God, did. Not because he felt anything for her but because he wanted the persistent widow to leave him alone.

"If this is the case with a human judge," Jesus concluded, "how much more will God, who loves you, hear and answer your prayers?" (See Luke 18:1–8.)

Perhaps like me, you too have felt like that widow, pounding on the doors and windows of heaven: "Get justice for me!"

During my year of religious, daily supplication, it seemed like God was the divine version of that unjust judge. It was easy to believe in those moments my heavenly Father was harsh, unfeeling, and needed to be pestered into doing what was best for me. That is not what this parable teaches us.

Jesus's point was that God is nothing like the unjust judge. Think about all the character flaws that judge had: he was a godless, apathetic hermit, wanting nothing more than to be left alone. God is the opposite: He is holy and wholly active. He desires our fellowship, loves us sacrificially, and is actively seeking our good. If even this judge—who hated God and people—granted the widow's request, how confident, how joyful, how comforted can we be in our requests to God? We are assured God will answer our prayers ("yes" may be the only answer we like, but there are other answers) and do what is best for us.

During my yearlong quest to beat down the doors of heaven, I didn't grasp that truth. Instead, I invested my emotional energy and time in repeatedly begging God to "show everyone my loyalty to purity isn't misplaced. Vindicate my faith. Prove You are right and that You reward right by giving me my husband!"

God answered my prayer and didn't give me a husband or children. Instead, He did something better: He let my dreams die. As marriage and kids became unlikely or even impossible, their lack created a painful void in my heart and in my life that I thought was going to be permanent. But gently, in the place of my dreams, God steadily built a memorial to Himself. That scarred part of my heart is now my strongest evidence that God is faithful and is keeping every one of His promises to me.

It wasn't the way I wanted, but God heard and responded to my persistent prayers. He reminded me Jesus Christ is my Bridegroom. We are engaged. Our wedding feast is ready and waiting. And eternity is our honeymoon. This relationship is so complete and fulfilling that no human marriage will be in heaven—and no one will miss it. We will rejoin our Creator in perfect unity. There may be no earthly husband involved, no children or idyllic home, but God will get justice for me.

That is reality for every child of God: we have a forever home, married to Christ and adopted as God's daughters. And praise God—He doesn't require a bride test the way some cultures do.

Traditionally, Mrs. Yazzie told me, Navajo brides must pass a bride test administered by the groom's mother to prove their suitability as a daughter-in-law. Before Mrs. Yazzie could marry Mr. Yazzie, she had to make fry bread for her prospective mother-in-law, who had wisely chosen the easiest thing for a *bilagaana* (white) woman to make. The older Mrs. Yazzie could have asked her potential daughter-in-law to butcher and dress a sheep, make *ach'íí'* (sheep intestines), or weave a two-gray-hills or a tree-of-life blanket. But she would have failed those.

That's why God doesn't ask us for a bride test. Because no matter how easy it might be, we could not pass.

For many years I was intent on the goal of marriage and family to the point of missing real life. I prayed and evaluated every man at every opportunity. I practiced and was skilled at running a home. I diligently prepared to raise a passel of kids. My time and career were dedicated to our future—even though an *us* didn't (and doesn't) exist.

I was deeply committed to my imagined earthly marriage and possible family. But I was only half-heartedly devoted to my heavenly marriage, only tangentially engaged with my spiritual family. Today is the day for this widow to wake up and move beyond "Get justice for me!" to "I rejoice in Your justice!" God has provided me a Husband. He has given me children. He has set me in a family. It doesn't look the way I thought or imagined, but my dreams are being fulfilled.

Our marriage to Christ not only exists right now and will last forever, but it comes complete with a Father, brothers, sisters, and children. God has not designed us to be alone spiritually or physically. By ourselves we are vulnerable to attack and lies, discouragement and doubt. In His loving wisdom, He has placed the solitary in families. This Yahweh-fearing family stretches all the way around the globe and spans all of human history. Every branch shares the vision to see the knowledge of God's glory fill the earth (Habakkuk 2:14), and all nations serve the Lord (Psalm 72:11).

God has given us the opportunities and skills (spiritual gifts) to plug into this family of God, called the church, where we have an irreplaceable role. Together we speak His words, teach His ways, and worship His name. We serve as God's hands to comfort the hurting and His feet to seek out the lost. Together, we are steadfast in trial (1 Peter 5:9) and agile in our wrestlings (Ephesians 6:12). We—the body of Christ—are the light of the world (Matthew 5:14).

Our family is worth investing in.

> ## It's time to step up and be sold out in our pursuit of God and our spiritual family.

And our family needs us; it needs our passion and our focus. We are the bride of Christ. Are we single-mindedly devoted to our heavenly Bridegroom, who gave Himself for us? We are mothers in the faith, called to encourage and nurture the faith of others. Are we consistently discipling our "children"?

It's time to step up and be sold out in our pursuit of God and our spiritual family. It's time to prepare, practice, and be the spiritual mothers we are called to be.

REFLECT

How can you more fully engage in your church as a mother in the faith?

PRAY

Talk to God about your dreams for the future and His dreams for you today.

TAKE A SINGLE STEP

Fulfill your calling. If you are not already, become involved in one ministry at your church that either builds up Christ's bride (the church) or disciples the children of God.

CONFESSIONS

OF THE

MIND

You will keep him in perfect peace,
Whose mind is stayed on You,
Because he trusts in You.

ISAIAH 26:3

Confession 9

BEWARE THE MATCHMAKERS

JANE LICKED HER LIPS, TASTING the long, tender grasses. She loved her life on the dude ranch. She sunbathed, splashed in the creek, and enjoyed being with the herd just like any other horse.

But Jane knew she was no longer any other horse. In fact, everyone knew it because her horn was now a full twelve inches, and it was not only pink, but glittery. That horn was a problem.

🐎

One, two, three . . . Oh, don't mind me. I am just counting the number of people who have suggested/tried/offered to set me up. I think I am somewhere around thirty.

You see, I have a problem. Typically, wedding photos grace the mantel of your first home. So if you're single, what do you substitute? Pictures of you and your dog?

Everyone at the emergency department (probably like your office) is always talking about their husbands, boyfriends, and kids. Evenings after work are reserved for dating and joyful rendezvous with significant others . . . unless you're single. Then having a dog only goes so far (and having a cat is no help at all). People, especially our brothers and sisters in Christ, know being directionless, isolated, and purposeless are all problems. And since many people equate being single to being lost, lonely, and loveless, they want to help. (*Loveless* is not technically a synonym for *purposeless*, but I really wanted an *L* word, and sometimes we equate lack of romantic love to lack of purpose.)

From total strangers to close friends, there are many people who would like to see us happily married. Everyone is so kind and thoughtful and . . . creative. I have had similar discussions with both sexes among my young married friends, my older married friends, and even some older single friends. In my experience these conversations run the gamut from suggesting ways I could meet X, to inviting X to have a meal with us without my knowledge, to wistful comments about how X needs someone like me.

It's cute. But the truth is, these conversations scare me to pieces.

"I have a son—I'll introduce you. He just got out of jail, so he's available!" Thank the Lord, I don't remember who made this suggestion, when they made it, or what exactly they said.

Even though I do want to be married, it always makes me nervous when people attempt to help me with my "single problem."

Numerous friends, acquaintances, and superficial contacts have numerous reasons why numerous friends, sons, friends' sons, and son's friends would be perfect for me. Normally, it is easily deduced that *perfect* is likely a slight overstatement. Ten years older, ten years younger, serial careers in fast food, has three children by three different women (and he is just an innocent bystander), or lost in life and taking applications for a navigator. Most of the time, it's an unfortunately easy judgment call.

You can see why matchmaking makes me nervous.

But what really scares me are Christian friends who are so fixated on me achieving the pinnacle of life—that is, getting married—that they want me to do any or all of the following:

1. Consider relationships with men who either aren't Christians or are stunted Christians. (ALERT! ALERT! ALERT! Disaster Dead Ahead!)
2. Date around to give myself the best chance at meeting a godly man. (Is this really what a godly man does with his time?)
3. Stop being so picky. (You are just going to be spending the rest of your life with this man—don't sweat it!)
4. Shorten my skirt, wear "that" a little tighter, and just let men know I am available. (Because that is sure to attract the right kind of men, lay the foundation for a solid Christian marriage and ministry . . . um, no.)

The underlying lie to all this advice is that getting married is the goal of life. Something to check off the accomplishment list. But it isn't, and it shouldn't be. The goal of every Christian's life is Christ.

He is the ultimate matchmaker, and in comparison, all other matchmakers straight up scare me because I scare me.

I am easily deceived and influenced by what I want to hear and believe.

For many years being single was, secretly, my number one life-imploding crisis.

My reasoning followed these lines: being lonely wasn't good, and that stemmed from being single. Being aimless was bad, and that came from being single. Being excluded from groups was hurtful, and if I were married, that wouldn't be the case. (Though, you wouldn't be able to go to singles' events, so that doesn't follow too well.)

The point is, I had (I thought) found the root cause of all struggles in my life: the lack of a significant other. I could and did write detailed lists of how marriage would fulfill me as a person, how it would complete me as a woman, and how it would open up avenues of ministry for my life. If I could just get married, *everything* would be solved.

God, however, never seemed impressed with my lists—because

they were wrong. They were based on the faulty premise that marriage fixes and fulfills everything. In reality, only Jesus fixes and fulfills everything. And I admit, I had been told this many times in various ways. My mother tried to tell me. Christian speakers tried to tell me. God's Word kept pointing it out. Even my friends' failed relationships were screaming the truth at me. And it still took decades before I could truly hear what they were telling me.

"You have an idol—it's marriage. And God won't put up with it."

Idols promise to give us what we want, when we want it, no strings attached. They lie. That's the truth.

God promises to give us what is best for us, at the right time, as we submit everything to His lordship. In His love, God is righteously jealous for our hearts. He will not sit by apathetically and watch us worship other gods—be they marriage, body image, or cars. God is actively training us, through the blessings He gives and the ones He withholds, to make us more and more like Christ.

It took many years for this reality to penetrate my weak, wayward heart. Not because I didn't know the truth. My head had known these things since childhood. But because I lusted for something other than God to complete me and make me whole and valuable.

This tendency still lurks in my traitorous heart, and to this day it is too easy for me to flip the switch in my heart from God to marriage. It tends to flip when I feel lonely or insecure. These emotions are easily triggered (such as by conversations about finding a husband), and it is a simple matter to allow my love and loyalty for God to be transferred to my old idol. Once there I am willing to pay any price to lay hold of a husband and family.

In those moments, I am vulnerable. If a matchmaker caught me then, I would be trapped like a rat, helpless as an upside-down turtle stuffed and mounted like a . . . you get the idea. I could be persuaded away from the goal for which Christ has laid hold of me (Philippians 3:12).

When I am focused on Christ, I don't fear waiting for the rest of my life if it be His will.

I have been waiting for Him to bring me to a man (like Eve to Adam) for twenty years. And guess what? God has been doing a great job with my life. When I am focused on Christ, I don't fear waiting for the rest of my life if it be His will. And I cannot speak for you, but I know my weakness. If my gaze slips off Christ, I am in peril of growing impatient and unwise and pursuing a man and passion that were not meant to be mine.

That scares me.

I've read the Book. The punishment for foolishness in relationships is far reaching and broad. If I choose the way of the fool (Proverbs 12:15), those consequences are all mine. And I am foolish enough already; I don't need any help. Instead, I need encouragement to trust God and lay hold of that prize for which Christ Jesus has laid hold of me.

I used to watch the Olympics obsessively, even the boring events, like long-distance running. Several times the top three runners were all from Kenya. A Kenyan friend of mine told me almost all Kenya's runners are from the same tribe. I was astounded and fascinated, because generally, the smaller the population, the smaller the chance at a medal. Except for this tribe apparently. But there is a simple explanation. Everyone in that tribe is a long-distance runner. That is what they do—they run.

There are different tribes in Christianity as well. Single Christians are a tribe. They are the patient tribe. They will win no medals, but that is what they do: they are called to follow God patiently.

People, myself included, sometimes look at me skeptically, expressions filled with worry. "Aren't you afraid of being alone . . . *forever?*"

Note the ominous italics on the word *forever*. Many people think deep down that if this is how it is right now, it will always be that way. If we are married now, we will *always* be. Or if we are not married now, we *never* will be. But neither is true. Marriage, like singleness, is a temporary blessing. People are always saying being married is hard and takes hard work. So I feel I can fairly confess being single takes work because it is hard. Being single is hard for one specific reason: we can fix the problem of being single, but instead we are commanded to be patient. And I don't know about you, but I hate being patient.

I am driven. Diligent. Determined. I have made things happen in my life.

And I don't want to do that with my husband or my marriage. Outside of asking Jesus to be our Lord and Savior, there is no more important decision than who we will marry.

Simply count the number of dating websites, singles groups at the various churches, and the number of single male coworkers we have. It would be easy to pick up a boyfriend. We know this because friends and acquaintances have successfully found partners, and—excuse the bluntness—we've all seen friends marry losers. But hey, they fixed their problem. The cost? Just a lifetime of regret. They wanted to marry and have a family. So they did. And they didn't want to wait for God's timing, so they didn't. And they wanted what they wanted, right now. And they got it.

I don't want that, and my guess is you don't either.

A quick flip through the Bible will demonstrate you can do anything you want if you put your mind to it. And this philosophy is an American birthright. But as Christians, what if there are times you shouldn't just go get what you want?

Abraham and Sarah created a physical heir for Abraham . . . disaster.

Rebekah made sure Jacob got the blessing of the firstborn . . . what a fiasco.

And then there is the debacle when Saul got tired of waiting for Samuel to offer the sacrifice and did it himself, only to lose the kingdom.

As you may have picked up on, patience does not come naturally to many people. My grandmother used to blame my red hair. But I think this is just a trait of humanity as a whole.

Who wants to wait to earn enough money to buy that doodad? No one. That's why we borrow.

Who wants to wait to have sex? No one. That's why so many children are born out of wedlock.

Who wants to wait for snail mail? No one. That's why we have email and streaming services and overnight delivery.

Fast food, drive-throughs, microwaves, and double speed all exist because no one wants to wait.

But we who are single are waiting. We are waiting for something that may not come . . . unless we force it. We are waiting for what many of us want more than anything else . . . except, prayerfully, Jesus Christ Himself. And we are called to wait patiently and productively . . . so help us God.

So in answer to the question, "Yes, I am afraid of being seventy-five in a darkened, tiny house without another living soul . . . unless you count the thirty cats."

I admit it. Right now I am scared of that. (Perhaps we have this fear in common?)

But many years ago I made a decision that has saved me on multiple different fronts. I determined not to make my life choices ruled by fear but rather to make them in faith. Faith makes decisions in light of God, His strength, His glory, His will, and His eternal kingdom.

You see, I have a conundrum (much bigger than the picture to put on my mantel). I fear being alone, but I also fear marrying the wrong person. I am scared of not getting married, but (if you catch me at the right time) I am also scared of all the changes marriage brings. I worry about never having children and in the same breath worry about the evil world they will inherit and the conniving influences they will face.

> Marriage can't fix our fears,
> but God can.

If you haven't caught it yet, I fear many things. Most of us do.

Marriage can't fix our fears, but God can. Focusing on Him quiets our worries and reveals the truth. In the presence of God, we don't need to fear being alone because God is always with us. And we need not dread the future, for we know we have a sure hope and eternal reward in heaven.

If we can trust God (and we can), if it is safe to put faith in Him (and it is), if He is the Lord God Almighty (and this is surely true), we can be patiently courageous. We never have to give in to impatience or worry. And with His help, I won't. How about you?

REFLECT

Is there something you believe will satisfy you and give you the life you have always wanted? Is that an idol?

PRAY

Open yourself up to God. Ask Him to show you anything in your life that is taking His place.

——— TAKE A SINGLE STEP ———

Fear doesn't have to run (or ruin) your life. Today, start one habit that will protect you from caving to fear. This might be something like repeating a Bible verse, saying a prayer when anxious, or doing one thing a week that scares you (for example, asking for forgiveness or talking to others about Jesus).

Confession 10

PATIENCE, MY FIRST LOVE

PATIENCE WAS A BLACK-AND-WHITE GUINEA pig that was always happy to see me. Her piercing whistles of pleasure could be heard in every corner of the house. When she first came into my life, I fed her fresh food every day and made it a point to cuddle with her just as frequently. I kept her water clean, her food bowl full (this probably explained her weight), and her crate newly papered. She was so cute!

But slowly the novelty of having a rodent friend wore off. She was still cute, but I became too busy to pet her every day. Feeding looked more like tossing vegetables in her general direction. And her cage now had to begin to stink before I would intervene.

My twelve-year-old soul had something in common with the Ephesian church—we both lost our first love. (You can laugh—it's okay. A childhood pet is the closest thing I can compare a first love to. But stay on point.) From hot to cold is the common story of human love. Unless carefully tended, our love for Christ can slip into this same pattern.

In Christian circles we tend to view love as purely an act of will or choice. Yet in Revelation 2:1–7, Jesus commends the Ephesians for their labor, patience, loathing of evil, discernment, perseverance, and strength.

Their choices were overwhelmingly good. Yet none of those good choices kept their love from growing cold. Everything looked okay—even excellent—from the outside, but their heart toward God was not as it should've been.

A single person does not have the luxury of hiding their waning love for God in love for a spouse or children. And as Paul reminds us, this focus is a gift (1 Corinthians 7). The first question of the Westminster Shorter Catechism is "What is the chief end of man?"

Answer? "Man's chief end is to glorify God, and to enjoy him forever."[1]

Man includes not only male and female but married and single. All of us are first and foremost created to know and enjoy God forever, and singles have fewer distractions to lead them away from Christ—if we so choose. That is a first love: ignoring distractions in order to focus our energy on the One who matters more.

Our culture tends to think of love as an emotional state outside of our control. However, Christ's admonition to the Ephesians is a command to return to their first love. If you can command something, it is clearly a choice. Thus, a first love is not only a feeling.

But if a first love isn't merely outward duties and it isn't just a feeling, what is it? Well, why couldn't it be both? Why couldn't it be Christ-centered action coupled with a heart on fire for Christ? I don't have it, but that's the love I want.

Jesus would not have commanded something that was impossible. Therefore, we know it is possible to regain a first love. But how? The answer to that question is a challenge for all Christians because no one's love is perfect, except God's. Let's look through a few strategies to protect and recapture our first love.

Pray

Our journey back to our first love begins with prayer. The Scriptures do not leave us self-deluded. We don't love God because of some innate goodness in ourselves. We love Him because He first loved us (1 John 4:19), and we continue to love Him by His grace and His Spirit. So asking Him to revive our love is a logical starting point. We don't have to want to love Him more . . . yet. We just need to be willing to ask God to help us love Him and want to love Him as He is worthy of being loved.

Make Time

When a couple first dates, no one has to tell them to spend time together. We understand no one can love anyone unless they make space and time in their life for that person. Just like plants in the desert die without fastidious watering, relationships in this sin-ridden world die without fastidious investment of time and effort.

Why would our relationship with God be any different? We must block out time to be with God one-on-one and jealously guard that time against intruders. "Lord, this time is Yours. No cell phone. No alarms. No entertainment. Just You and me."

Plan and Make It Exciting

Have you ever found yourself at the end of your quiet time saying, "Well, God, I sat here for fifteen minutes, and You said nothing, so I'm going now"? Not many of us would invite a friend over just to stare at each other before saying goodbye. That is not satisfying for anyone. But we do that with God and then seem surprised when our devotions with God are not satisfying either.

God is not boring. Our time with God can be exciting because He is captivating. We don't have to speed-read three chapters, say a rote prayer, and call it good. We can vary what and how much we read of God's Word. We can pray and study in different ways and at different times. We can even sing, write, or draw our biblical meditations.

Include Him Always

Seventeenth-century lay monk Brother Lawrence said, "Let us occupy ourselves entirely in knowing God."[2]

God is not confined to a part of our morning or a snippet of our evening. He wants to be (and we want Him to be) integral to our entire day. Every Christian has the opportunity to welcome Him into their lives continually. Christ deserves to be foremost when we go to work, do chores, hang out with friends. Jesus is the one we serve in everything we do (Colossians 3:17). But singles are blessed to be able to do all to the glory of God with a laser-like focus.

Avoid Distractions and Choose Accountability

"How do you like the new stucco?" My dad was the facilities manager where we lived.

"It's nice. How did you decide on the colors?" We were curious.

"Picked them out of the catalog." He smiled. "I got a couple different shades of brown."

"Uh, Dad?" We looked at each other. "Some of the houses are green."

Dad's eyes grew round, and he blinked. "I didn't have time to ask."

You see, my dad is color-blind. Being in a hurry, he had not asked his secretary about his color selections. Knowing his perspective does not reflect reality, he is generally careful to get someone else to approve color choices before committing to them—except in this instance.

When it comes to evaluating ourselves, our perspective does not always match reality either. We have a hard time seeing our imperfections. It is important to be willing to ask a mature Christian friend, "Am I distracted by things that don't matter?"

Just as everyone needs a checkup now and then—someone to keep us accountable for our physical health—everyone needs spiritual checkups too, with someone to prod us to make healthy spiritual choices and encourage us when we just don't want to do X anymore.

Choosing such a friend to be a sounding board is humbling and uncomfortable. It can't be someone who is a busybody or just too busy, period. It needs to be another woman courageous enough to tell you the truth and kind enough that you want to listen. She has to be actively desiring to grow personally and willing to ask how your walk with Jesus is growing. And it always bears asking, "Would I be a good friend for others to ask for accountability?"

Be Grateful and Focus on the Positive

Growing up with a military father, I would often hear my mother say, "You can live anywhere for two years." Meaning no matter where my dad was transferred, we could make it. But in our relationship with Christ, we want so much more than to just make it—we want to hit it out of the park. A pivotal element to enjoying a relationship (or a new duty station) is focusing on the good things and being grateful for them. If we are always harping on our mistakes in our pursuit of God, or complaining that God isn't doing what we want, or trying to manipulate God into doing things our way, we will grow discouraged because we are focusing on *ourselves* rather than on our good and gracious God.

Get a "Like" Makeover

In any good relationship both parties learn to like what the other likes. In regaining our first love, we should learn what God likes. Indulge in conversation with Him. Listen to music that glorifies Him. Meditate on things that bring Him pleasure. Establishing daily habits that make God's desires inherent within our lives is part of restoring our first love.

As we grow closer to God, we come to enjoy those things He enjoys and are able to see how He is blessing our lives. Much of this revelation takes place as we purpose to tell ourselves the truth.

Tell Yourself the Truth

We let ourselves believe lies all the time. We watch our favorite programs or favorite sports teams because we tell ourselves it will make us happy. We need to tell ourselves the truth. The truth is, God alone gives us joy. He makes life fulfilling. He is everything we need. Our relationship with Him is the best thing this life offers, and we get to indulge it every day in so many ways.

You know the sad thing about my guinea pig? She was a rodent, and rodents don't live long, especially when they get a dental infection. One day Patience wasn't doing well, and the next she was gone, and with her went any chance I had to rekindle my first love. There will not always be tomorrow to love God. A last hour will come. And "because we have such a short time to live, we should spend our remaining time with God."[3]

—— REFLECT ——

Think about your first human (or pet) love. What aspects of that experience speak to your relationship with God?

—— PRAY ——

Pray through a passage of Scripture—like Isaiah 64:1–5; Jeremiah 31:1–14; or Revelation 5:8–14—and write down each of the truths presented in it. Thank the Lord for being your first love.

—— TAKE A SINGLE STEP ——

God is love, and He is your love. Make or do something special just for Him today.

Confession 11

YOU SHOULD HAVE BEEN MINE

MEET ALISHA'S CRUSHES. NAMES HAVE been changed to protect the innocent, the guilty, and the embarrassed.

Al. Al was the cutest guy in the first grade. He had straight blond hair cut in a bowl shape—trendy at the time. We went to school for a whole year together, and then one of my friends told Al I liked him, and poof—no more crush.

Paul. Paul was the kid down the street. He had straight brown hair and, again, a bowl haircut. Paul was funny and always had something to say. Then he moved away, and we saw each other a couple times after that, but I guess he always saw me as the chubby redheaded girl next door.

Phil. Phil was younger than me, so I thought he was short, but his athleticism more than made up for it. And of course, he had . . . a bowl haircut. He was smart and always good for an intellectual debate. As we got older, though, his adventurous spirit got him into trouble with girls and with God.

Will. Will just happened to come on the scene right during the time I realized I was in real danger of never getting married. He didn't have a bowl haircut, but boy, was he built. He loved God, respected my dad, and wanted a military career. But I guess the attraction was one-sided.

Raul. Raul was not Hispanic (but I couldn't come up with another name that ends in *L*). He was my one celebrity crush. For years I admired his courage and his character. I once told my family I wanted to marry a man like him. My brother didn't miss a beat. "Why not just marry him?" He then went back to eating, as though this were a perfectly sane recommendation. Years later I see this as a compliment, but it still makes me laugh.

All those crushes, but I only ever had one boyfriend. His name was Caleb. And you can only keep reading if you promise not to think I am too weird.

Even though we were little more than toddlers when we first met, Caleb and I grew into being good friends. After I moved across the country, we sent each other letters in huge, wobbly handwriting, and he sent me a bracelet. What makes that even sweeter is Caleb was pretty sick at the time with leukemia. Shortly after we moved, Caleb died. We were seven.

I know it is an odd, somewhat morbid and fanciful notion. But I have often wondered, *What if he was my soulmate?*

Most people think of soulmates as a purely romantic notion. In other words, soulmates are a nice idea that doesn't translate into reality. This is the sentiment even inside the church. I have heard multiple pastors say "the perfect one" for you doesn't exist. Thus, as long as he is a Christian and she is a Christian, it is okay—God will somehow make it work.

I used to think this as well. So it's not that I am a devotee (emotionally or otherwise) to the idea of soulmates. And it's not that I think there is one for me, because at this point I have to think that the odds are not in my favor. But I am unashamedly devoted to an all-knowing, all-powerful, and all-loving God. God knows everything, so by definition there is nothing hidden from Him. That means He knows exactly who the best person is for you. Thus, there must be one man in the world who by comparison is the best husband for you—that is, your soulmate.

"But even if there is," I've heard people say, "how can you be sure you will meet them?"

Or alternatively, "That is too much pressure, trying to pick the exact right person."

Well, God can do everything—there is nothing too hard for Him. Water to wine, He can do that. Using a fish as transportation, no problem. Defeating a whole army with three hundred men, no trouble. So orchestrating a romantic introduction is no problem for Him. (In fact, He's done it: Adam and Eve, Isaac and Rebekah, Boaz and Ruth . . .) He's even straight up told people, "This is who you should marry" (see Matthew 1:20).

And God is good, so all His works and plans are good also. Therefore, He will bring His children the best partner, at the best time, and let them know at the best moment. Thus, based on the character of God, I am firmly convinced and maintain soulmates exist and are worth waiting for, even if mine never comes. Which is a difficult pill to swallow as a self-centered, impatient person. I work in the emergency department. I did college in three years. I microwave everything on high. All because I am an inherently impatient person bent on achieving my goals . . . quickly! So I make my next point honestly, as a person who recognizes her own faults reflected in the lives of others.

People don't want to believe in soulmates because then the wise (and the obedient) will wait for them. But if soulmates are a figment of a romantic imagination somewhere, why wait? Only a fool waits for what does not exist. And, bottom line, even within the church, we don't want to wait for God's soulmate for us. So we get around this inconvenience by denying their existence.

Then we are free to seek out a mate on our own, unfettered by God's timeline. And that's awesome since His timeline seems to be littered with words like *stop* and *wait* and *stay*. But what people don't realize is that God's timeline for us still exists—separate and regardless of the existence of soulmates.

Believe in soulmates or not, but God is still God and still gets to say, "Not now." Which is also a tough pill for a self-centered, impatient person, especially when "not now" is beginning to look like "never."

As I search the Scriptures, I have come to believe that the call to Christian singleness is a matter of obedience and submission to the will of the Father. Unfortunately, I see many refusing God's call to be single because being single is a hard gift.

A hard gift is one that has bitterness mixed in with the sweet. But a godly observer would still understand it as a gift. Let me give an example.

Years ago, I had a patient in preterm labor.

The doctors had already told her the baby had a genetic abnormality that was usually fatal. He was going to be born with numerous medical and mental handicaps. His mother had been planning to have a second-term abortion because in New Mexico you can do that. But God intervened, and instead she went into labor early.

She delivered a little boy, who lived out his hours surrounded by family. He was baptized by the family priest, and even in the sorrow, she was rescued from the shame and guilt. She had done everything she could. She could freely mourn her child—instead of sweeping him under the rug. Her family could now support and cry with her—instead of being torn over her decision. She was provided a path to sorrow untainted by regret.

That is a hard gift. But—like singleness—it is still a gift.

Because singleness is a gift, we who have been given it should be grateful rather than merely looking to break it and get a new one. We can be grateful because God is good. And we can joyfully follow His timeline because our Savior is seeking our best, whether our gift is for one year, ten years, or one hundred years.

REFLECT

What do you think about soulmates? Given the character of God, are they possible?

PRAY

Ask God to work on your weakest character trait. And expect Him to do so.

TAKE A SINGLE STEP

How is your singleness a hard gift? For every answer to that question, give an answer to this question: How is your singleness a holy gift?

Confession 12

HELD IN HONOR

YOU'VE PROBABLY SEEN MONUMENT VALLEY, Arizona, even if you didn't know it, because numerous movies have been shot there. Monument Valley is famous for its red mitten-shaped rock formations. It has great hiking and crazy four-wheeling. If you have never fishtailed around sandy corners in a VW van driven by a young-at-heart missionary, you are totally missing out. But more importantly, at least to me, Monument Valley was the location of the first wedding I helped with.

One homeschool mom and five homeschool girls drove up the night before the event to decorate the church. We bowed, crafted, and arranged. Then we hung pew bows, fussed over the décor, and pretended not to watch the rehearsal.

We couldn't help but be curious about what would happen. We surreptitiously watched the couple practice coming down the aisle. We vaguely listened to the pastor's instructions.

Then the line came: "You may now kiss the bride." And we couldn't pretend not to be listening anymore, all eyes riveted on the front of the church. Everybody knew: this couple had never kissed before.

Twelve: That's how old I was at that wedding.

Fifteen: Three short years later was the first time I thought, *I could legally get married now.*

Eighteen: This year was the first time I felt ready to get married and said so. Whether that feeling was based in reality or imagination, you be the judge.

Twenty-one: In my mind, that was the perfect age to get married.

Twenty-five: I agreed with Harriet from *Emma.* "You will be an old maid! And that's so dreadful!"[1] By the time you reached this advanced age, you were dried up. Why even bother getting married if you had the chance (which you wouldn't)?

Some foolish. Some practical. Some ridiculous. I thought, said, and wrote all these things and many more about marriage, getting married, and being married.

"Marriage is an honorable institution. Created by God." Years later, I listened carefully as an officiating pastor spoke. "And is representative of Christ and His church."

At a cerebral level, I knew these things. But I didn't understand them. It took many years for my mind (and the Holy Spirit) to flesh out the reality about marriage the way God ordered it.

Marriage Is a Sacred Relationship

As temporal beings, we tend to see marriage as a God-established human relationship. And marriage is God's by design and possession, but it's not merely a human interaction.

When a Christian bride and groom stand before the congregation, they are not up there alone (and I am not talking about the pastor or the attendants). God stands with them because marriage initiates another person into the most personal bond any of us possess, and it's not the one with our mothers. Marriage brings a third person into our relationship with Jesus Christ. It is a sacred relationship between a woman and God and a man.

Overwhelmingly, people see marriage as a physical and emotional relationship. But it's more than that.

Dennis Rainey says, "Marriage first and foremost is a spiritual relationship. . . . If you push the spiritual dimension to the side, you are ignoring the very God who created marriage and the One who can help you make it work."[2] So many marriages (even in the church) fail because they ignore the spiritual and are based on physical intimacy and emotional ties. This is also why marrying a non-Christian or a wayward Christian is spiritually devastating. And this is the reason the Scriptures speak so strongly against such unions and urge us to understand and respect marriage as a platform for God's purposes.

Marriage Is a Purposeful Relationship

"There's a reason for everything Alisha does," my friend once said. And I'll admit that I wish that were true, but it's not always accurate.

The crowds who reported that Jesus "has done all things well" (Mark 7:37) nailed it because, "As for God, His way is perfect" (Psalm 18:30). Nothing He does or commands is capricious or purposeless. Therefore, as the workmanship of God, singles have purpose, and marriage, as designed by God, also has functions.

Genesis 2:18—Provide companionship and partnership

Do you think God was surprised when Adam couldn't find a suitable helpmeet? No, of course not. So if there is a reason for everything God does, what was the purpose of this naming-the-animals exercise? God was forcing Adam (and us) to realize something was missing in paradise. He was also displaying His love and miraculous ability to provide whatever is necessary in the moment. And thus God created Eve and marriage to perfectly fill the void.

If God could do this for Adam (when there were no women in existence!), is He not also fully able to do this for you and me? And if He chooses not to, does He not have a worthwhile reason?

Hosea 1:2—Display God's faithful love

Basically the first thing God said to Hosea was "Go marry a whore. Your wife will demonstrate how Israel is treating me. And you must love her faithfully, as I love Israel." Marriage is a drama of God's faithful love toward people who do not deserve it. During their lifetime, both husband and wife will have ample opportunity to display this unconditional love.

If God could demand Hosea marry an unfaithful woman and have an eternal reason for it, could He also request that we not marry and have an eternal reason for it?

Malachi 2:15—Produce godly offspring

Dishonor within a marriage damages one's relationship with God. These implications are fascinating and more than a little fearful. God says His goal for demanding fidelity and kindness in marriage is unity for the purpose of raising up children who are sold-out to Him.

> Is it not rational to believe that God expects all believers to be unified in faithful love so we are able to raise up spiritual children?

If God so clearly requires this within marriage, can we not reasonably conclude this is what He desires from His relationship with His church? Is it not rational to believe that God expects all believers to be unified in faithful love so we are able to raise up spiritual children?

1 Corinthians 7:1–2—Promote purity

"Better to marry than burn" is such a pervasive sentiment that even non-Christians have quoted it to me. But Paul's instructions concerning using marriage to protect our purity show clearly that he considered using marriage this way as a concession, not a celebration. Why?! This is every teenager's favorite purpose for marriage! Exactly. This is a reason for marriage. But if it is your only reason, the marriage will be crippled, and it will struggle to fulfill God's other purposes.

If God provides marriage to protect us from our sinful desires, can He not also provide a way of escape to those of us who remain unmarried (1 Corinthians 10:13)?

Ephesians 5:22–27—Exhibit Christ's relationship with the church

If being married doesn't sound hard enough yet, it's about to get harder. Rob Jackson with Focus on the Family comments, "Our marriages are icons of the sacred union between Christ and the church."[3] When God established marriage, He knew humans would sin, destroy His creation, and need a suffering Savior to restore perfection. He foresaw Christ's sacrificial relationship with His church and said, "That's how marriage should look."

If God knew from the beginning that marriage would be a picture of Christ and the church, does He not also know how a single can show forth the glory of her God and Savior?

Marriage Is a Blessing, Not a Right

I am not entitled to get married. God does not owe me a man.

No, marriage is God's, like I am God's. It is used for His purposes to advance His kingdom and for our enjoyment. Thus, in the marriages of His children, God gets the final say.

This is not what we see in our churches, let alone in our culture. God is pushed out of the process of wooing a spouse. Then at the wedding we ask for God's blessings. Why would we expect this to work? Maybe it's because we do not hold marriage (or its Creator) in high enough esteem.

God's design for the marriage relationship, and the intimacy of it, reflects God's dealings with us, His church. And beyond this, when man and woman are bonded together, they enter into a holy institution, loved by God. This is why Hebrews says whether we are married or single, marriage and the privileges thereof are to be held in honor by all. "Marriage is honorable among all, and the bed undefiled; but fornicators and adulterers God will judge" (Hebrews 13:4).

Clearly the author is speaking specifically of physical intimacy, and yet I believe he also speaks more broadly about the relationship of marriage.

When a married couple is physically intimate, they hold marriage in honor. When a single person is abstinent, they hold marriage in honor. As a married couple lives together in unity and joy, they respect the God-given glory of marriage. And as a spinster lives in contentment and devotion to God, she respects the God-given glory of marriage. When a husband romances his wife just as when a single man chooses to avoid superficial relationships, they honor marriage. As a wife respects and supports her husband and as a single woman prays for and supports married friends, they respect marriage.

Single, widowed, married, engaged—we honor marriage together as the body of Christ. To the Lord we do or do not do all these things, as a bride whose deepest desire and purpose is to honor her Bridegroom.

As we understand more of God's purposes and design for marriage, it becomes easier to understand the opposite side of the coin: singleness. What were originally plausible opinions on singleness become obvious misconceptions in the light of God's Word.

Common Myths About Christian Singles and Singlehood

The first common myth about Christian singles and singlehood—*Your marital status shows your inherent spirituality*. The irony is that some think singles are more spiritual and others think married folks are. But God warns us against comparison (2 Corinthians 10:12). Spiritual people are marked by their character and service, not their marital status (1 Corinthians 2:13–14; Galatians 6:1–3).

Numbers 2 and 3—*There is something wrong with them because they are single, or they did something wrong.* Since all of us are sinners, both of these things are true. But they do not explain why we are single. For followers of Jesus, all our sins have been washed away and no longer define who we are or what we do (1 Corinthians 6:9–11).

Number 4—*They want to be single.* Maybe. Maybe not. But this is beside the point. Christians lay down our lives to take up our cross and follow Christ, whether He leads us to marriage or not.

Number 5—*Singles are unhappy.* We don't have to be. The joy of the Lord is our strength (Nehemiah 8:10—and the man who said that was single!).

Number 6—*Singles and married people have nothing in common.* This is a lie. We have everything in common that eternally matters. One body. One Spirit. One hope. One Lord. One faith. One God. (See Ephesians 4:4–6.)

Number 7—*Singles are immature and free of obligations or responsibilities.* God does not agree. Regardless of relationship status, His children all are tasked with the responsibility to "Go . . . and make disciples of all the nations" (Matthew 28:19).

Number 8—*Singleness is a problem.* Next to self, sin, death, hell, and Satan—singleness doesn't even make the list.

Number 9—*Singles need help to fix their problem of singleness.* God sees singleness as an asset, and there is no problem that requires skills God does not have.

Number 10—*Singles will eventually get married . . . because everyone does.* This is not what Jesus taught. For various reasons, some are and will continue to be single for the kingdom of God (Matthew 19:12).

A Christian couple is not married because they are spiritual or mature or beautiful. They are married to honor Jesus Christ. All other reasons are so far down the list that they truly don't matter. Christian spinsters are not single because we are spiritual or immature or weird—though these things may all be true! We are single for the honor and glory of Jesus Christ.

PS: The couple in the opening story didn't kiss during the rehearsal either—just in case you were wondering.

REFLECT

What blows your mind when it comes to how God designed marriage? If God put that much effort into marriage, which will cease to exist in heaven, can you be sure He has put that much effort into His plans for you? Your soul is eternal.

PRAY

Worship God for His masterful plans for the planet, your nation, your church, and yourself.

TAKE A SINGLE STEP

We just spent nearly a whole chapter looking at God's goals and blueprints for marriage. Now let's spend a few minutes looking at His design for being single. As you do this, fill in the chart on the opposite page. God's purposes and plans are not confined to marriage.

References for Being Married

Genesis 2:18

Hosea 1:2

Malachi 2:15

1 Corinthians 7:1–2

Ephesians 5:22–27

Purposes for Being Married

Provide companionship and partnership

Display God's faithful love

Produce godly offspring

Promote purity

Exhibit Christ's relationship with the church

References for Being Single

1 Corinthians 7:27

1 Corinthians 7:29

1 Corinthians 7:32

1 Corinthians 7:34

1 Corinthians 7:35

Purposes for Being Single

Have contentment and freedom

Confession 13

A UNICORN AMONG HORSES

"WHAT ARE YOU DOING?" A kind voice interrupted Jane's failing efforts.

"I'm trying to get rid of my horn." Jane sniffed.

"With mud?" The owner of the ranch smiled gently.

"Yes!" Jane wailed, and a piece of mud-encrusted mane smacked her in the face.

The man tried not to laugh at his unicorn who was rolling in the mud. "It looks like you made quite a mess."

Jane nodded, and a tear cleaned a trail down her dirty cheek. "I don't know what else to do. I tried covering it with my mane. But that looked . . ."

"Silly?" the rancher supplied.

Jane nodded. "And I tried wearing a medieval hat."

"One of the pointy ones?" The man cracked a smile.

She nodded again. "But it kept sliding down over my eyes."

"I bet it did. So tell me, why are you trying to hide your horn? I think it's beautiful." He rubbed the dried mud off her face.

"Because it's a neon sign saying, JANE ISN'T A HORSE. And everyone treats me differently."

"Why do you think people treat you differently?"

Jane snorted. "It's the horn. It's pink and sparkly, and no one can take their eyes off it." That was an easy question.

"Maybe that's because you can't keep your mind off it." He patted her neck. "Maybe others focus on it because you focus on it."

Jane almost stomped her hoof. "I can't just forget about it! It's a log sticking out of my skull."

"Well, you know what I see when I look at you?" He didn't wait for her to answer. "I see four hooves that are good for trail riding. I see a broad chest, great for pulling. And I see strong hips, perfect for carrying a rider. Just like all the other horses." Jane's owner smiled until he had her attention. "You want to go for a ride?"

Jane shrugged and wiped a tear away on his vest.

He grinned. "And you know what?"

"What?" Jane sniffed.

"Only a unicorn can give me . . . this!" He rubbed his hand down her horn and threw a handful of glitter into the air.

Jane giggled. "You know that stuff gets everywhere!"

If your church is like mine, it is easy to feel like a unicorn in a pasture of horses. Everyone else is married, having children or grandchildren, doing the expected Christian-life things . . . except for us. Thank goodness we don't have pink glittery horns. But we do have glitter: something singles can give God that married people cannot.

For me, this realization started with my least favorite Bible verse. (If you don't have a least favorite Bible verse, don't feel the need to go looking for one.) And my least favorite Bible verse is appropriately found in my longtime least favorite chapter of the Bible: 1 Corinthians 7. I don't dislike all of it, of course. The sections on marriage are awesome! It's the parts about singleness I find . . . distasteful. (A recent epiphany for me was that married people may not like this chapter much either, but for the opposite reasons than mine!)

"But I say to the unmarried and to the widows: It is good for them if they remain even as I am" (1 Corinthians 7:8).

This begs the question: How was Paul? Single. Perpetually single. *Big sigh.*

And to make it worse, he describes singleness as a gift (verse 7). Talk about the worst Christmas present ever, like getting cleaning supplies or wrinkle cream.

But no matter how bad (or amazing) a gift is, Christmas in our family means we want to see you open it, so we open presents one at a time. Christmas morning takes hours, and we often wade through gifts in increments for days or even weeks. So consider yourself warned if you ever spend Christmas with us.

Part of our fun is informally guessing what a package may contain. It doesn't take long after you've done it for a few years. Books, puzzles, and clothes are easy to guess, unless they are disguised. But if you know (or think you know) what is inside a package, it is easy to become biased about which gifts are good and which ones are bad. After all, no one wants to get socks and underwear for Christmas. So packages with something that feels like clothes may be ignored in favor of the packages that look like jewelry (or books, in my case).

First Corinthians 7:7 says as far as relationships are concerned, everyone gets a gift from God. Some get married and some stay single, but both are gifts from God.

Singleness is one of those presents that feels like socks, and so few people ever want to open it. The problem is that all clothes feel the same, and until you open a gift you can't tell if it is underwear or that dress you've had your eye on. First Corinthians 7 unwraps the gift of singleness and transparently compares it with marriage. But you have to be willing to open the gift.

My least favorite chapter in the Bible was written in answer to a question Paul was asked by the Corinthian church about marriage, singleness, and serving God. But we don't know exactly what the question was. So it is a bit like hearing one side of a conversation. (All the important parts are there though—scout's honor.) And if you realize this, it isn't surprising that Paul jumps right to the conclusion in verse 1: "It is good for a man not to touch a woman." But if you stop there, it is like ignoring a present because the bow is ugly. The next forty verses parse out the apostle's teaching and reasoning behind his conclusion.

Throughout this chapter Paul lays out three goals for the church as a whole: sexual purity, contentment, and wholehearted service to God. Then he outlines strategies to help married members and single members attain those ends.

Goal 1: Sexual Purity

Married Strategy: Commit to each other for life (and have sex)
Single Strategy: Exercise self-control

My grandmother was famous for wrapping everything and giving all the kids identical gifts so no one could complain. One Christmas we found these beautiful round tubes under the tree and, keeping with family tradition, immediately shook them, trying to figure out what they could be. She told us not to shake them. And of course, we asked, "Why? Will they break?" To which she mysteriously replied, "Yes, but it won't hurt them." What?! Our pediatric minds were baffled, until we opened the tubes on Christmas morning to find potato chip . . . crumbs.

As a seaport, Corinth was famous for its sexual sin, and shamefully, the church was too (1 Corinthians 5:1). Thus, it is insightful that Paul's first goal was sexual morality (1 Corinthians 7:1–2). The married do this, Paul says, by realizing their bodies belong fully to their spouse and giving themselves to each other without reservation (verses 3–4). As the monk married to the nun (aka Martin Luther) once said, "No man is so virtuous as to marry a wife only to have children."[1]

Couples control their passions by being faithful to their spouse and committing to their marriages for life (verse 11). This is the gift of marriage. (Singleness seems less hard when compared to the finality of marriage done God's way, doesn't it?)

The unmarried maintain sexual purity by exercising self-control and ruling over their passions (verse 9). This is the gift of singleness.

Goal 2: Contentment

Married Strategy: Live married and free in Christ
Single Strategy: Live free as a slave of Christ

At the core, every gift God gives us is good (James 1:17), but He feels no compulsion to make everything He gives us look enticing. Unlike my grandma, God is not compelled to give all His children the same gifts. This is why Paul spends verses 17–24 in 1 Corinthians 7 on his second goal, contentment.

"Who do I inbound to, Coach?" The overeager player looked like a rabid squirrel.

The coach smiled. "Whoever you want to. Just get it to one of our players."

The squirrel bounded off to the basketball sideline.

"So why don't you ever say that to me?" One of the more seasoned players looked amused.

"Because"—the coach gestured at the game clock—"you play when there is more than 0.67 seconds left on the clock."

In 1 Corinthians 7, Paul, like the coach, was eyeing the clock. In both cases the time was short—so short the coach realized the inbound didn't matter, and Paul argues that neither do our life circumstances (verses 29–31).

Now, if you are thinking, *They matter to me*, I am right there with you. But think about what serious business was when you were three years old—ice cream was high on my list. How much does that matter to you today? In heaven we will have an even fuller perspective than we have now of our childish priorities. Though it is hard to imagine, in heaven marriage will be a thing of the past and won't be anyone's defining feature anymore. As we see more clearly how right Paul was about our time and service to God on earth (verse 35), the question of whether we marry or not will be like ice cream. It's nice if you have it, but it's not a priority. And this is where we finally get the reason for Paul's abrupt conclusion in verse 1.

Slave or free, circumcised or uncircumcised, married or single, God does not see these life circumstances as obstacles to our faith. On the contrary, from His eternal perspective, these are gifts to allow us to do the only thing that really matters: obey the will of God (verse 19). One of those commands is not to worry about your economic status, your skin color, your nationality, or whether or not you are in a relationship (verse 21–22). Instead, contentedly abide in God (verse 24). Discontentment (like shaking potato chips) mars even the best of situations.

Goal 3: Wholehearted Service to God
Married Strategy: Serve God through serving your spouse
Single Strategy: Focus fully on the things of God

Here is where the rubber meets the road. Paul starts the chapter by arguing celibacy is better but ends the discussion with his strongest argument for remaining single.

Those who are married have to care about serving their spouse and their family (verses 33–34). And from a practical and God-honoring standpoint, they should. This is their God-given privilege and responsibility (1 Timothy 5:8).

But those who are unmarried have no such obligations and are free to please God (1 Corinthians 7:32). This is why Tony Evans, a preacher and founder of the Urban Alternative, says, "Being single is more desirable for a Christian than being married."[2] Those who are celibate are able to focus on the things of God (verse 34) and to present themselves to God as holy in spirit and body. Do singles always do this? No. But only in singleness does the possibility exist for this level of passionate service and devotion to God.

> Our calling is to be devoted slaves of Jesus, ready and willing to serve however our Savior desires.

This is God's command to us, His singles. Our calling is to be devoted slaves of Jesus, ready and willing to serve however our Savior desires. In our current state, and by God's grace, each of us has the capacity to make eternal investments in God's kingdom. This is the true gift of singleness.

But it is always our choice. We can choose to concentrate on what we do not have: companionship, children, a secure future. Or we can choose to focus on what we do have: time, energy, and a personal invitation from God to serve Him wholeheartedly. As we choose the latter, we glean an extra measure of joy as we get to experience the wonderful blessings God has for us (verse 40).

Please pause here and consider these truths. Depending on where you are, 1 Corinthians 7 can be difficult to believe. When we are hurting, distracted, or discouraged, it is hard, even humanly impossible, to respond appropriately to what God is saying.

But the facts remain. God is pleased with your singleness because He sees the potential for His relationship with you to deepen and bear fruit. Our Lord is glorified by your singleness in a unique way that is only possible because you are single. He is planning to use your singleness to grow His church and benefit His kingdom. And those possibilities exponentially expand as you choose to live in holiness, grasp His contentment, and seize your mission to serve Christ.

REFLECT

Our gift of singleness is one of holiness, freedom, purpose, and joy. What keeps you from being grateful for your gift?

PRAY

Thank God for His design of the gift of singleness, and praise Him that it is a good gift for you (even if you don't understand how it is good yet).

TAKE A SINGLE STEP

On a full-size sheet of paper, write down the three goals Paul had for the church. Decorate it any way you want and post it somewhere you won't lose it. (You are going to need it in future chapters!)

Confession 14

MADE FOR THIS

Isn't it fascinating what your computer thinks you want to learn about? In one particular week the same topic came across my feed multiple times: pastors and speakers marveling about marriage as a picture of Christ and the church. Mentioned consistently (by married individuals) was their amazement that marriage as a sexual union also displays the relationship of Christ and the church. They were embarrassed by this intimation. They were in awe of it and, frankly, a little baffled.

Here, I realized something: married people do not have a corner on the knowledge market. Everyone is always saying things like "If you were married, you would understand" or "When you have a husband, you'll get it." And they are right, of course. But single people know things and have the potential to understand certain things at a deeper level.

From the beginning it was clear it was not good for man to be alone. Even in the perfection of the garden of Eden, he was designed for marriage. Eve was created specifically for the purpose of being a helper, a companion, and a lover. Her body, heart, and spirit were prepared to bear and raise children, just as Adam was designed to father and protect those children. So why will some of us never fulfill God's obvious design for our sex?

Let me introduce you to one of my family's favorite words: *puzzling* (verb).

Definition of *puzzling*: the act of putting a puzzle together (minimum five hundred pieces).

Many things in life are puzzles. They seem out of place until you find their other half. As soon as they click into place, you know they are designed to fit each other like a plug in an outlet, a screw and a screwdriver, or . . . male and female.

The body of a man and the body of a woman were clearly designed for each other. They are obviously made as the complement to the other, to complete the other, to enjoy the other, and to bear godly offspring. My body is made for a man, and yet sex is not for me right now. And as every unmarried person is acutely aware, it may never be.

Never is a long time. And one feeling that isn't often addressed is, *Isn't it unfair of God to give me desires that cannot be or haven't been righteously satisfied?* People all over our culture are asking variations of this question. Why am I attracted to this person who is not my spouse if it is wrong? If it is a sin, why am I interested in people of the same sex? Why am I unhappy as a female (or male) if God made me this way?

Too often, instead of digging for the answers, we just presume God is at fault. But starting today let us assume God is true, and every person (including us) is a liar (Romans 3:4). If we believe God, who never lies (Numbers 23:19), when we come across a question or a problem we do not understand, we know the problem resides with us. Maybe our mind is reasoning incorrectly or with incomplete information. (God cannot make either of these mistakes by the way—Isaiah 55:9.) Perhaps our emotions (our hearts) are deceiving us (Jeremiah 17:9). Or less flatteringly, maybe our sinful desires are dragging our minds and hearts to hell (James 1:13–14 and 4:1).

Now, let's ask the question again. If God made me, isn't it unjust of God to give me desires I can't satisfy if I am obeying His law?

Well, God did make us, and not only did He make us, but He did a good job. Psalm 139:13–14 is clear on this point. Since God is perfect, He cannot be unjust (Habakkuk 1:13) or show favoritism (Romans 2:11). But we are not perfect, so something must have happened to make us the way we are. What happened is sin. We are rebels against God and His laws (Romans 3:23), and that rebellious attitude inside us drives our appetites (Romans 7:18–19). Thus, we have lusts that cannot be fulfilled while pleasing God.

When God created us, He put inside us core desires. These core desires can be righteously satisfied. Unfortunately, in our sinfulness, we twist these core desires away from what God intended and into what "self" says is good. And anything we twist is bound to go badly.

Observe: everyone has a desire to be securely loved. This core desire is designed to turn our hearts toward God as the only Perfect Lover. But we often try to fulfill this desire by getting married to a perfect lover, having serial sexual relationships, or indulging in pornography or other addictions.

The latter three we call sin. The core desire to be loved is still there (and it is good), but it is left unfulfilled as we ravenously try to satisfy our lust for love and security.

Since God is the only Perfect Lover, the expectation to find and marry a perfect lover is an idol—an impostor scheming to assume Christ's role in our lives. Recognizing this can be incredibly difficult because marriage is a good thing, a natural thing, a gift of God. Only an individual can really say if they are making marriage or relationships with the opposite sex an idol and allowing it to compete with God for lordship of their life.

But now we have found the real question: What do I do about these desires I cannot righteously fulfill?

When we identify a desire that cannot be fulfilled in a God-honoring way, we need to take it before God and trace it back to what our heart is truly seeking. That core desire can be satisfied righteously. For example, am I struggling to resist a married man's advances because I crave affirmation? Or am I engaging in serial shallow relationships because I need acceptance?

The Bible tells us God has made us with inherent value. We are His people made in His image for His purposes (Ephesians 2:10). Jumping into bed with some guy or dating compulsively won't give us value, but believing the truth will. Because while our bodies are half a puzzle made for a man, our spirits and souls were made for God. They are a complement of Him. In Christ we are complete (Colossians 2:10) and our core desires are fulfilled. We are accepted. We are loved. We are safe. We have an eternal future.

"In the resurrection . . . whose wife will she be?" The Sadducees' question in Mark 12:23 was about a woman who was married to seven brothers, each of whom died before leaving an heir.

Jesus was nonplussed. "They neither marry nor are given in marriage . . . in heaven" (verse 25).

Since Scripture is clear that sex is exclusively reserved for one man and one woman who are married for life, this conversation leaves the honest observer with several conclusions about heaven. First, there is no marriage. Second, there is no sex (which is enough to send a significant portion of the population into a panic).

At our core, our Creator has designed us for marriage . . . to Himself. In heaven, the Bridegroom's relationship with His bride (us) is fully consummated (pay attention to this word). Right now we live with the promise of that marriage: we are betrothed to our beloved. But in heaven, we will be face-to-face, hand in hand with our Savior and our God. Our marriage will be fully realized as an all-consuming relationship, so rich and beautiful we will neither need nor desire human intimacy: emotional, mental, spiritual, or physical. And especially when it comes to the physical, some people are floored. "No marriage. How can that possibly be?"

Subby Szterszky, managing editor of the *Focus on Faith and Culture* newsletter, notes, "For many believers who are serious about the Scriptures, this qualifies as one of those 'difficult sayings' of Jesus."[1]

But you and I know. Here in this evil, marred world, married couples have a partner. Their future is together. Our future is alone. That stark isolation opens a crack into heaven, through which we taste the truth: God is enough.

A true relationship with God satisfies at a spiritual level—deeper than mental agreement, emotional closeness, or physical contact. It is the act of the Creator reconnecting with His creation and the creation—you and me—responding, "Yes, Lord. I was indeed made for this." Within this relationship we are who we are meant to be, the bride of Christ, purposed to make disciples (godly offspring).

The Bible calls all Christ-followers to fulfill the same design: to be married to Christ and disciple "children" in the faith. So whether we marry or not, bear children or not, God is holding out His grace to completely fulfill His design for us and for our sex.

The strength of our relationship with Jesus is the linchpin to self-control in the single life.

We have experienced this truth in a way our married brothers and sisters by definition cannot. They may have tasted sexual unity and then come to the same conclusion: only God is enough. But we who are single believe God. And based on who He is, His Word, and His promises, by faith we conclude intimacy with Christ is even better than taking a human lover.

Not simply enough to survive or get by, but He is enough to satisfy the true cravings of our hearts. We know how much we want to marry, but if we don't marry, we know God is enough. And if we do marry, God is still enough. We don't need sex. We don't have to have physical children. But we have to have God.

The strength of our relationship with Jesus is the linchpin to self-control in the single life. When Jesus's words and wonderful works fill our minds, sinful daydreams and fantasies cannot flourish.

"But in a great house there are not only vessels of gold and silver, but also of wood and clay, some for honor and some for dishonor. Therefore, if anyone cleanses himself from the latter, he will be a vessel for honor, sanctified and useful for the Master, prepared for every good work" (2 Timothy 2:20–21). As Jesus takes first priority in our lives, our physical appetites come under His authority. And as we surrender to Jesus those desires—that at times seem all consuming— we become vessels for honor, holy and fitting for the Master's use.

REFLECT

Where do you struggle most with self-control? How can you protect yourself from this temptation? (Consider something like praying for the salvation of others whenever you are tempted.)

PRAY

Express to God your desire to live a self-controlled life for His glory (or request that He give you this desire).

TAKE A SINGLE STEP

Take your list of goals from 1 Corinthians 7. The first one is sexual purity, which for an unmarried person is achieved through self-control. Write down one specific, personal goal you have for self-control. Include a strategy to help you attain that goal; it doesn't have to be elaborate. Avoiding the computer, using a filter or an accountability app, finding an accountability friend, and refusing to continue reading books or watching movies or shows that awaken those appetites are all possibilities.

Confession 15

IN NEED OF AND IN RESPONSE TO GRACE

"Hey, Nate!" Dave offered his friend an iced tea with a little umbrella as he came out onto the patio. "I've been thinking."

"About what?" Nate lowered himself onto the chair next to Dave.

"My house."

Nate raised his eyebrows. "Your house?"

"Yeah—look at this place." Dave waved at the building behind him.

Nate nodded. "It's big."

"Big and luxurious. Who would have ever thought a sheep rancher's son would live in a place like this?" Dave sighed and settled back.

"It is pretty amazing. God sure has blessed you."

"Exactly!" Dave looked at Nate through his huge sunglasses. "That's what I was thinking! God needs a house. And I want to build Him one."

Nate savored his tea. "That sounds like a great idea. I can't wait to see what you come up with, my friend."

Dave laughed.

Nate drained the tea. "I should go. It looks like dinner's coming." He motioned to a gaggle of servants at the patio door. "Enjoy your evening."

Dave may have enjoyed his evening, but Nate didn't get much sleep because God had a few things He needed both Nate and Dave to be aware of.

The next day, the prophet Nathan had to go tell King David no.

God's response to David is twelve verses long (2 Samuel 7:5–16), and it is intriguing—both what was said and what was not.

God did not belittle David's desire to build the temple. Instead, He gently reminded David, if the King of creation had wanted a house for Himself, He would have asked. God reiterated that David was called to shepherd a kingdom, not build a place of worship. And in the end, even though David desired to give God more than the tabernacle, God was asking for a different sacrifice.

For those of us who want to marry and raise up a household of children for God, this is important to hear. God will ask from us what He wills for us. He isn't playing hide-and-go-seek or expecting from us what we cannot give. If He doesn't provide a husband or children, He is not asking us for a godly marriage or children. Instead, He must be desiring a different sacrifice, and that sacrifice may require everything we have. To live is Christ, and to die is gain (Philippians 1:21).

Lesson 1: God will treasure our dreams of bringing Him a great gift, but often He will change our plans.

The Holy One of Israel did not laugh at David's plans. God is the Lord of heaven and earth, and it cannot contain Him. Certainly no house of ours will be sufficient to contain Him—no matter how much gold or silver or stone. Everything we give God is from Him. There is nothing we can give grand enough to impress Him, nor is there anything we can supply without Him (Psalm 50:12).

Growing up, we loved to play garage sale at my grandparents' house (we tried it at home, but it was never quite as successful). We would scour the basement for small items to sell to my parents and grandparents for five or ten cents. It was the best game ever. We sold them back their own stuff, and they paid us for it!

We are doing the same with God. Every breath we take is from His hand and for His good pleasure. We serve Him only through His enabling. And though we think of our service to God as a gift to God from us, in reality everything is His already—including our singleness. David realized quickly that he was playing garage sale with God, and it brought him to his knees. The God who spoke the universe into existence graciously listened as David offered to give Him back what He already owned. (This would be a good place to pause and worship God for His incredible humility, grace, and love.)

Lesson 2: God will give us what we need in order to give Him exactly what He wants.

It is particularly instructive to notice the Lord did not humor David's idea and let him think/do what he wanted without intervention. David's God-given purpose was to lead the people of Israel as king. God knew David's years were flying by and would soon be over (Psalm 144:4). The Ancient of Days wasn't going to silently stand by and let David waste his life doing anything other than what God designed for him to do. And God won't let us waste our lives either—if we are willing to accept His instruction.

How we use our time equates to how we use our life. For those of us with regrets in our past (1 Peter 4:3), don't despair. Our God is the author of our days and the redeemer of our souls. He is able to restore to us in wondrous ways what is absent or destroyed because He alone is God (Joel 2:25–27). In Christ our lives have been redeemed; to spend our current lives on anything other than what God wills for us is a waste. Whether we are single or married, it is God who reveals to us His will and brings us into it.

Lesson 3: God guides us into His will.

In response to these eleven verses, the king after God's own heart said, "Who am I, O Lord GOD . . . that You have brought me this far?" (2 Samuel 7:18).

David may have missed Paul by a millennium, but both concurred: "But by the grace of God I am what I am, and His grace toward me was not in vain; but I labored more abundantly than they all, yet not I, but the grace of God which was with me" (1 Corinthians 15:10).

God's grace to be content is likewise abundantly provided to us today.

Did you ever make those origami paper or fortune-teller games that were supposed to show you who you would marry when you grew up? You know—the ones you folded and put on your fingers and opened and closed them a particular number of times. I have, and I was very lucky at them: I got married every time! (There's not an option to remain single.) Though, I will say the one time we played in high school, one of the guys got married to three of us . . . so clearly not the best indicator of the future.

We were all about sixteen. Some of us had savings accounts, but most of us had blown the entire balance on a car or clothes. The lion's share of us hadn't a clue what we wanted to study in college, let alone where we wanted to go to college. But all of us were planning on getting married. And most of us were planning on having kids. Even in our young minds, education, career, and finances were clearly less important than a spouse and children. (God isn't on the list because the cohort I am referring to was largely secular.) Fast-forward a few years, and the future is here. We can all look at that list of priorities, and we know how well we've achieved them. Any boxes checked are by the grace of God. He has provided the opportunities, the intellect, the physical stamina, and the heart to accomplish those things (Deuteronomy 8:18). Any boxes not yet checked are blank also by the grace of God. For by the grace of God, I am what I am.

Resting in this—the grace of God—contentment is not only possible but inescapable. King David found this out as God reviewed his life. Who chose him? Who protected him from Saul? Who kept David from killing Saul or Nabal? Who established him as king over Israel? Who blessed him on the battlefield? Why did a shepherd have a name among the great men of earth? God. Only God.

If we were to write questions for everything good in our lives, we would find the answer to our questions is the same as David's. God. Only God.

This is a humbling realization, and once it sinks down into our core, we will join David on his knees in awe and gratefulness: Who am I that you've brought me this far?

REFLECT

In what areas of your life do you struggle with contentment? Why?

PRAY

Worship God for His great goodness toward you.

TAKE A SINGLE STEP

Take your list of goals from 1 Corinthians 7. The middle one is contentment. Write down one personal goal you have for contentment. Include a strategy to help you attain that goal—like thanking God for something in that area of your life every day or memorizing a verse to refocus yourself when you envy someone else.

Confession 16

PLAYING THE UNICORN

"I KEEP STANDING AROUND—BUT no one notices me. And"—Jane carried her master around the last bend before the barn—"if they do notice me, they don't know what to do with me."

She took a breath, knowing she sounded whiny. "I like going on rides and pulling sleighs and even helping with plowing! But no one ever picks me."

The owner of the dude ranch chewed on a piece of hay. "Well, are you standing in the stable? That's where all the horses who want to go to work are."

Jane wrinkled her nose. "Sometimes."

"Ah. Well, I know you are interested—do you look interested?" He dismounted and grabbed a brush.

"How do I look interested?"

"Poke your nose out of your stall and tilt your ears forward. Then when a cowboy comes by, whinny or nuzzle his hat." The rancher laughed. "That works most of the time. Have you done that?"

Jane squirmed. "Kind of."

"Of course, the easiest way to get out of the pasture is to just vol-

unteer." He patted her haunches. "And it looks like you'll get to practice. Something's happening at the barn."

🐉

At some point, you probably had a phase where you felt like Jane. For
me it was during my awkward phase between college and grad school
(as compared to my many other awkward phases in life). I went to the
young adult Bible studies, and I looked, mostly, like I belonged there.
But the truth was, I wasn't young anymore. My life experience was
far different from the just-out-of-high-school crowd, which was most
of the group, and vastly different from the leaders who were married
with small children.

As I look back, I realize the young adult crew was essentially a
stand-alone church inside a church. The married couple who led were
up to their necks in service with music and kids ministry, but the
singles were disconnected. Some of them continued to hang around
with the youth group (because they weren't invited anywhere else),
and the rest were only vaguely attached to the church body.

I would have immensely preferred to have been part of the wom-
en's groups. I wanted to be included in ministries with older Christians who had more life experience. I wanted to attend Bible studies
with people who would actually talk about things of substance. But
I was never invited, and at that time in my life, with my reserved
personality, no invitation was the same thing as a closed door. Thus,
for several years, though I faithfully attended church and events, and
even helped family members with things they had volunteered for, I
felt completely isolated in my pew seat.

And no one really knew. Perhaps you can relate. (Or better yet,
maybe you can't.)

At the time I thought it was 80–90 percent our church's fault.

They hadn't invited the young women into their women's ministry. They hadn't worked to include us in the life of the church. They failed to reach out to those without families. They neglected to ask singles to serve.

With these thoughts pouring through my brain, I tried a different church for six months. Then while I was in PA school, I attended an additional two churches for a year and a half. But the setup was universally the same! Married couples with children leading a small, segregated group for the church's singles. Still minimal interaction with the main body. Still no invitation to join the women's ministry. Still no request for me to serve in the church.

Disappointed, and a little cynical, I returned to my family's church and thought, *Yes, they should invite me. Yes, they should make room for me. Yes, they should reach out to me and give me a place to serve.*

But what is my responsibility?

Well, first off, it is to faithfully attend. But it is also incumbent upon me to love and encourage others in faith and service (see Hebrews 10:25).

You may find this difficult to believe, but I was an awkward, painfully shy preteen, especially in large groups. It was so bad that at church I would pretend to be intently reading the bulletin during the meet-and-greet time or would hang out in the kitchen to avoid speaking to anyone. (I found this was generally better than looking like I wanted to talk to people and then being passed over week after week.)

My mother used to tell me on a regular basis, "She who wants to have friends must herself be friendly." That did not make me happy. I wanted friends, but I didn't want to take the risk of being friendly. My ninth-grade year, my parents helped me take those risks and made me take speech and debate. As much as I am loath to admit it because I shed a lot of tears over that class, learning to speak publicly did make me less gawky. As I became more comfortable with myself and more confident that I had words worth saying, I found it easier to talk with others.

It was soon after this that I realized something else: my personality was only partially to blame for my shyness. The other part of my shyness was self-absorption. Whether we were at a party or at church, in my mind it was all about me. I wouldn't engage because I was too concerned about what people would think of me.

I understood this initially in high school, but God had to reteach me after college. My wallflower status at church was a result of disconnectedness within the church and my personality, but it was also evidence of my selfishness—I wanted to be sure I would be accepted before I would engage. And if I wasn't sure, I didn't do whatever that was. My attitude was "me first."

But as Christ-followers, our attitude is to be "you first" (Philippians 2:3–4 and Romans 12:10). This is especially true within the church—we are to love, comfort, care, serve, and submit to one another (John 15:12; 1 Corinthians 12:25; Ephesians 5:21; 1 Thessalonians 4:18). The church does not exist to serve us but rather for us to serve God and others as a unit.

This means it is our responsibility to take the announcements about church functions as invitations and not demand others invite us personally before we will act. It is our responsibility to attend and find out where we fit, not simply wait for someone else to put us in the game. (God already did this when He gave us salvation through faith in Jesus Christ.) If we want to be part of the women's ministry, it falls on us to volunteer. If we want to help in children's, prison, or homeless ministry, we need to offer to serve.

It's easy to hide behind "it's the church's fault," but even if it's true—and sometimes it is—before God we are only responsible for us. We can only address our shortcomings. When we don't engage in our local church, we lose. We miss out on the comfort and encouragement of godly friendships with saints of different ages. We make ourselves more vulnerable to temptation, discouragement, and apathy. We squander opportunities to fulfill God's purposes in our lives. And most importantly we stiff-arm God, who has chosen to work through the church as His body (Ephesians 1:22–23).

What sets us apart as singles—our gift from God—is the time, energy, and ability to focus fully on Christ and His kingdom. This gift is designed to be used within God's church. To refuse to use God's gift is to reject God's will (Hebrews 12:25). Our choice to refrain from wholeheartedly joining Christ's body robs the church of our spiritual gifts and the good works God has prepared for us (Ephesians 2:10). But when we consciously insert ourselves into Christ's church—in our communities, on our military bases, or in the mission field—we are presenting ourselves to God as living stones to build up a holy temple to the Lord (Ephesians 2:19–22).

That is what you and I are striving for today and every day until Christ returns. At the end of time, our sacrifice and service is what we will lay before the throne of heaven (Philippians 2:17). May we be able to say, like the servant did in the parable of the talents in Matthew 25, "Master, You gave these gifts, and now, my Lord, I return them to You doubled."

REFLECT

What keeps you from serving wholeheartedly? Why?

PRAY

Review with God how you have used and are using your gifts (including singleness) for His glory.

—— TAKE A SINGLE STEP ——

Take your list of goals from 1 Corinthians 7. The last one is whole-hearted service to God. Write down one personal goal you have for serving God. Include a strategy to help you attain that goal. It may be asking where you can help or taking training to do ministry. It may be giving up TV shows or other time sucks in your life to serve more fully. It might be as simple as showing up, or maybe God is asking for something bigger, something much, much bigger.

CONFESSIONS

OF THE

FLESH

For this is the will of God, your sanctification: that you should abstain from sexual immorality; that each of you should know how to possess his own vessel in sanctification and honor, not in passion of lust, like the Gentiles who do not know God; that no one should take advantage of and defraud his brother in this matter.

1 THESSALONIANS 4:3–6

Confession 17

JANE'S HORN

"GO ON!" THE RANCHER GESTURED toward the barn where horses and cowboys gathered. "GO!"

Jane whimpered but obeyed his pointed finger and trotted over. She ignored the stares and inserted herself into the stable. She stuck her head, horn first, into where the ranch hands were talking.

"We've got a bunch of kids coming for the hayride tonight. And I figure we need three teams," the ranch foreman said.

Jane was so excited she forgot to nudge his hat, but she did whinny before he selected the first two horses. Jane watched expectantly, but she wasn't chosen for the second team either. Or the third. She felt the familiar slump of her ears and tail.

Then one of the cowboys frowned. He ran a gentle hand down the horse's back leg and shook his head.

"Blackie's pulled up lame."

As Blackie limped back to his stall, the dun, named Candy, stood there all alone. Jane looked at the empty space in the harness. She felt the rancher poke her. Taking a big gulp of air, Jane walked forward into the space next to Candy.

The cowboy came back. Jane felt jittery.

"Well, look at you!" He walked around, sizing up his newest team. Finally he nodded. "You'll make a fine pair."

Jane stood calmly even though she felt like dancing inside. Her ears flicked forward as she leaned into the yoke. They were almost out of the barnyard when her eyes grew wide: she hadn't thought about her horn at all.

She whinnied as her master flashed her a thumbs-up. She was made to do this job, and now she was doing it!

🐎

Review question: What color was Jane's horn?

If you said pink and glittery, you are absolutely correct! (Please feel free to write "100%" in the margin with a smiley face or fireworks or whatever tells you "I did a superb job!" And if you would like to figure out what color your horn is, check out the end of the chapter. Mine is lime green.)

Jane's horn was continually not only on her head but on her mind. That background conversation with herself influenced her choices and her emotions. Our singleness can become like a pink glitzy horn if we let it. Jane Austen was right: "A lady's imagination is very rapid; it jumps from admiration to love, from love to matrimony in a moment."[1] Whether I was going to camp or to a dance, volunteering for a fundraiser or attending a conference, for years the thought that I could find my husband pervaded. Since this was constantly in my mind, it is not a surprise that every man I met went through my mental decision grid.

Alisha's Decision Grid

Step 1: Determine: Is the subject married?

    Step 1A: Check for a ring.

Ring? Move to Step 1D.

No ring? Move to Step 1B.

Step 1B: Listen for the subject to mention wife or children.

Mention? Move to Step 1D.

No mention? Move to Step 1C.

Step 1C: Cleverly verify subject's relationship status. Suggested ways to do this under Step 1E.

In a relationship? Move to Step 1D.

Not in a relationship? Move to Step 2!

Step 1D: END DECISION GRID. NOT A PROSPECTIVE HUSBAND.

Step 1E: Suggested ways to verify subject's relationship status:

1. Ask about plans for upcoming holiday or the weekend.

2. Inquire who he came to the event with.

3. Ask how his family is doing.

4. Talk about pets (or just about any other subject) and ask what his wife thinks about their pet.

5. Come right out and ask. (Note: this is not clever.)

Step 2: Subject is unmarried. Evaluate for suitability as husband.

Step 2A: Calculate positive and negative points for dialogue (+10 or -10 points per). Move to Step 2B.

Step 2B: Calculate positive and negative points for actions (+10 or -10 points each). Move to Step 2C.

Step 2C: Add up all points. If the total is less than 50 points, go to Step 1D. If the total is more than 50, go to Step 2D.

Step 2D: SUBJECT MAY BE A POSSIBLE HUSBAND. INITIATE CONTINGENCY PLAN!

My mental habit was ingrained, and every new man I met went through this grid. The mental energy and the time it takes to evaluate every possible partner this way are substantial. And I knew that, but over the years God unveiled other costs to this practice.

Cost 1: The decision grid made everything all about me, my thoughts, my emotions, my opinions, my desires.

My habit convinced my subconscious that those men were there for me. Their sole purpose for existence in my part of time and space was to see if I might be interested in their companionship. It's hard to engage in friendship or work or ministry or much of anything if we allow our thoughts to revolve around us. If others are just there for us, we will fail to support them as we are called to as their sisters in Christ.

Cost 2: My brothers in Christ were reduced to subjects.

My practice seemed innocent until I realized I mentally was making men, who were supposed to be my brothers in Christ and fellow heirs and servants of God, into objects. They were merely things there for my pleasure, my taking or leaving. Objects don't have important opinions or emotions. They are valuable only inasmuch as they are desired. And they are easily replaced. If I view others as things, I am going to struggle to value them, be patient with them, respect them, or serve alongside them.

Cost 3: I was ineffective in service to God (or others) because I was too busy strategizing to get what I wanted.

I was too distracted—assessing to see if *he* was what I wanted. And I was too self-consumed—making sure *I* didn't miss what I wanted. At a cerebral level, I knew my grid approach was damaging my relationships with others and God. I knew it was feeding "me" and not pleasing God. But I would tell myself, "How else am I going to ensure that I don't miss God's guy for me?"

Part of me really wanted to serve God (but it was a smaller part of me than I thought). So I did all the things for God and kept my grid readily accessible to screen for a husband. God started nudging me. "You know that grid thing you do—that's not good."

"But . . ." I argued with God (though I would have called it "discussed"). "I just do it the first time I meet them, so it's okay."

After years of the grid method, I grew discouraged because

1. I think I have met at least 78 percent of the Christian population in New Mexico;
2. I was getting older and getting nowhere; and
3. though I was reaching desperation, God was moving the exact same speed: virtually 0.0 mph.

But God, moving at His perfect speed, was getting somewhere in me. Bit by bit God was building up the part of me that desired Him and His will first, and just as slowly He was tearing down my commitment to me. And that was when He said, "That grid's got to go."

I finally agreed, but . . . how? I had to replace the grid with *something*, or this wasn't going to work. Prayer became that something. Every time I started using my grid again, that became the cue to pray for each man as a brother. One of the most efficient ways I found to do this was to pray for their future wife and ministry with her in their church and in their family. (It is amazing how quickly this shuts down daydreams about them as a potential husband.) Then instead of using their shortcomings to mark them off my list, I tried to make notes about these things with the intent of encouraging and supporting them.

As men around me lost their object status, I was able to see their strengths and envision how God may desire to use them in ministry. It incrementally grew easier to be happy for them as they got married and had children—wasn't that what I prayed for? As I saw them maturing and moving into ministry, I could now rejoice because, even though it wasn't with me, God was using them in great and awesome ways.

It's been almost twenty years, about ten of which I have been resisting the allure of the grid. And you want to know a secret? I still have to kill off my decision grid on a regular basis, often when I am least expecting it. But you want to know a bigger secret? After so much practice, it's getting easier. I found the way out that God always provides (1 Corinthians 10:13).

REFLECT

Do you reflexively put men through a decision grid or other process to evaluate their eligibility? Or shake their hand and imagine your future home, ministry, and children? If yes, how can you replace your thoughts with God's thoughts?

PRAY

Ask God to reveal to you any inappropriate thought patterns toward others that are damaging your relationships. This could include attitudes of competition toward other women or possessiveness toward men. It might be spending intense mental energy to gain male attention or approval.

TAKE A SINGLE STEP

Before you start thinking, *Could he be the one?* purpose to do something else, such as pray for him, recite a Bible verse, or listen to worship music.

Bonus! What Color Is Your Horn?

All unicorns have glitter, but question 1 tells you how much.

1. I tend to be more (pick one):
   A. Extroverted
   B. Introverted
   C. Equally extroverted and introverted

A unicorn's glitter is how she spreads joy to those around her. She does this by pursuing excellence, giving herself and others grace, and investing herself in those around her. Generally, the more extroverted you are, the more glitter you naturally have, but either way a wise unicorn consciously works on giving her glitter away.

Answer the next two questions and match them to the appropriate space in the table.

2. Of the choices below, the one that sounds most like me is . . .
   A. I have a fiery, upbeat personality.
   B. I am sincere and consistent.
   C. I am fun, funny, and maybe a bit bubbly.
   D. I am expressive and artistic.

3. Of the choices below, the one that sounds least like me is . . .
   A. I am a planner.
   B. I am easygoing and spontaneous.
   C. I am adventurous (and a bit of a daredevil).
   D. I am dignified.

	3A	3B	3C	3D
2A	AA—Pink	AB—Rose	AC—Russet	AD—Red
2B	BA—Turquoise	BB—Baby Blue	BC—Royal Blue	BD—Purple
2C	CA—Orange	CB—Burnt Orange	CC—Gold	CD—Canary Yellow
2D	DA—Sage	DB—Hunter Green	DC—Moss	DD—Lime Green

The Reds/Pinks

You are highly motivated, and many admire your confidence. You know all the tricks of influencing people positively and have what people call "a presence." No one ever doubts your sincerity.

Because of how motivated you are, it is easy to start caring more about what others think than what God thinks. Consistently model your character after Christ, and God will always be first in your heart.

Theme verse is Philippians 2:3–4: "Let nothing be done through selfish ambition or conceit, but in lowliness of mind let each esteem others better than himself. Let each of you look out not only for his own interests, but also for the interests of others."

The Blues/Purples

What you see is what you get. There is nothing underhanded about you. You are a loyal friend. You make life choices carefully, and your well-rounded personality lets you and everyone around you enjoy life.

Your straightforward nature tends to make you think you can do it alone. Being consciously reliant on God and grateful for the people He has given you will help you avoid this.

Theme verse is Psalm 63:8: "My soul follows close behind You; Your right hand upholds me."

The Yellows/Oranges

Your humor and bubbly demeanor make you the life of the party. And your energy is infectious to everyone around you. Your creative mind keeps you, your friends, and your family from ever being bored, and there are few things you don't enjoy.

Since you like new things, you can be a bit rash and have a hard time finding and finishing what really matters. So taking time to seek God before making decisions will serve you well in all areas of life.

Theme verse is Ephesians 5:17: "Therefore do not be unwise, but understand what the will of the Lord is."

The Greens

You would describe yourself as having an artistic soul. You are excellent at expressing your ideas and have more than your share of an intelligence spark. In general, you feel life deeply, even if you tend to be a bit reserved.

This can cause you to become wrapped up in yourself. So keep your eyes on Jesus and make it a priority to focus on Him every day. He is Life and His Word brings light.

Theme verse is Hebrews 12:2: "Looking unto Jesus, the author and finisher of our faith, who for the joy that was set before Him endured the cross, despising the shame, and has sat down at the right hand of the throne of God."

Confession 18

DID SHE REALLY JUST ASK THAT?! (PART 1)

OUR SOCIETY, AS JUDGED BY our entertainment, thinks the only good thing about being a virgin is that, in the event of spell casting, you may be able to fulfill some magical or mystical role, such as providing your blood, becoming a human sacrifice, or being able to see the future.

Christ's community, though, should have a more mature and sober perspective on the importance and blessings of purity. (I am not just talking about not getting sexually transmitted diseases, cervical cancer, genital warts, and so on. Though God does bless our obedience in many ways, including the intensely practical, and we should not minimize those rewards.) The question about the role of abstinence in the lives of individuals in church affects the church as a whole. The topic is especially cogent to those of us who, enabled and called by God, live celibate lives because they will know we are Christians by our love (John 13:35), both by love given and by love righteously withheld.

True love waits. We've heard the spiel a million times. But no one ever said it may have to wait for a lifetime. The True Love Waits lady in high school was specific about what not to do, but that can't be all love waits for . . . can it? Is marriage really that one-dimensional? No, right? We know marriage is an intimate, sacred relationship far deeper than simply sleeping with someone.

So virginity can't really be that one-dimensional either, right? But if it's not, what is virginity?

I hear you whispering, "Did she really just ask that!? Come on, this is embarrassing. Everyone knows what virginity is." Well, maybe not.

Most people think purity is purely about physical intimacy. And further, most people, when discussing or considering this topic, restrict virginity to the act of having sex. But broadly speaking, virginity is the state of not having done a certain thing (until you finally do that thing for the first time).

Do you remember your first day of school? Your first movie? Your first airplane flight?

Firsts are special. And those who take part in our firsts are special. My first movie was *The Prince of Egypt*. And decades later I still remember the movie, who was there, and the theater.

It was a good first movie.

I waited for that moment for nine long years. But there are many things in life we will wait much longer to do for the first time. When discussing virginity in the context of relationships, we know sex is off limits. But what everyone really wants to know is, How intimate can or should we be before marriage? But even that question is too narrow because we are not just physical beings. We have minds and emotions and souls. So it stands to reason that intellectual, emotional, and spiritual virginity exist. But how are we supposed to safeguard those for our spouse?

This is something I am still working through. But let's start with the easy one.

Physical Virginity

Here are the basics: sex is only for inside the box. The box is marriage as God defines it—one man, one woman for life. Any type of sex outside that box is sin (Galatians 5:19–21). But just as importantly, having sex is not the apex of life (even if our culture thinks it is). Sex is not even the most important aspect of marriage. The first spot in life and in marriage belongs only to Jesus Christ. Get it? Got it? Good.

So now that we've covered the basics, let's be honest: not all physical touch is intimacy. But a couple is physically intimate the instant they hold hands, hug or kiss, cuddle, dance, take off their clothing, or . . . you get the picture. Let's be even more honest: the Bible does not delineate *this is okay* and *this isn't*. However, God does give us guidance in order to build healthy relationships within the church.

Principle 1: God is always priority one.
God is always supposed to be number one in our lives. If anything is obstructing an open relationship with God—whether it is good, bad, or ugly—it needs to go.

The most nascent aspect of physical intimacy (and other types of virginity as well) is in the imagination. It is an unfortunate but common girlish pastime to daydream about boys and marriage and family. Guys, on the other hand, are more likely to visualize the physical aspects of the relationship rather than a home with a white picket fence. Either way, these mental exercises are founded on our imaginations, not reality. They often open a door to temptation today and disappointment tomorrow when our spouse (the real person, not the superman we've envisioned) inevitably fails to be our perfect, imagined spouse.

Once these kinds of harmful thought patterns become ingrained, they become like desert plants, which are nearly impossible to uproot.

You can't just burn off the tops or use weed killer; you have to put in the effort to dig up that tap root. I still remember the victory when I went to a function with thousands of people and only evaluated one man there for his suitability as a husband.

There is a lie out there that says as long as it doesn't hurt anyone, it's okay. People justify inappropriate daydreams, pornography, sex outside of marriage (before and after), and a host of other sexual practices this way. The truth is, these all hurt everyone involved, even if we don't think so. Impure practices take a participant's innocence, destabilize relationships, and create ugly addictions. They steal pleasure and exclusivity from marriage. And most importantly, they destroy one's focus on God.

Many people, both male and female, have this struggle; it's called lust. But the human tendency is to seek an outlet for these feelings instead of seeking God—the only source of lasting satisfaction. Daydreaming, addictions, relationships, and even marriage cannot and do not fix a lust problem, regardless of the degree of physical intimacy involved. In fact, as we allow deeper physicality in a relationship, we can awaken further appetites that cannot be righteously satisfied. But when God is central to a relationship, all conversations, all activities, and all desires are subject to His loving guidance.

God's commands to us are gifts to pull us into the best life possible because there is something (sin) and someone (Satan) pulling on the other side.

Principle 2: We live in a war zone, and so do our churches.

In our commitment to live holy lives, we are waging war, and our choices affect our brothers and sisters in Christ. As such, whether single, dating, or married (and hopefully still dating), we are actively on guard and fleeing sexual sin just like Joseph. Joseph didn't try to reason or pray his way out. He knew he wasn't strong enough to win this battle, and he was courageous enough to admit it. It is a prudent person who knows their weaknesses, strategizes to avoid those temptations, and plans in advance to take the way of escape as soon as God provides it (1 Corinthians 10:13).

A wise person sees evil coming and makes provisions (Proverbs 22:3).

Principle 3: Plan to avoid temptation.
Establishing boundaries protects us from our weaknesses.

When you are deciding what kinds of physical intimacy are acceptable in your relationships, seek wise counselors and consider with them the consequences for your relationship with Christ, your possible future marriage, and those around you. Is this decision setting the stage for sexual sin? Which of those firsts belong to your husband? Which ones do you want to enjoy only with him? What would you be okay with your husband doing with others before you are married?

Notice there is no table or pie chart. I cannot provide a handy-dandy cheat sheet of God-approved physical contact before marriage (or tell you what percentage of your romantic relationship should be physical in nature). I simply don't know.

However, I do know God is worthy of trust and will keep His promises (2 Corinthians 1:20). If we obey Him by keeping Jesus first, remaining vigilant against sin and Satan, and intentionally avoiding temptation, He will bless us (Deuteronomy 30:9–10), guide us into all truth (John 16:13), and sanctify us in Christ as His saints (1 Corinthians 1:2). (The Corinthians were notoriously surrounded by sexual immorality. If God could help them, He can help us.)

REFLECT

What lies do you believe about virginity or holiness? (Some common ones include holiness is boring; purity is outdated; I am missing out on the good stuff; God doesn't really care; I've already messed up too badly anyway; and it's a personal matter and doesn't affect anyone else.)

PRAY

Thank God for His sanctifying work in your life, and praise Him as God—holy, holy, holy—who fully forgives you and enables you to "walk worthy" of Jesus Christ (Colossians 1:10).

TAKE A SINGLE STEP

Take a piece of paper, and for each lie that you identified above, write the truth. I like to think of these truths as stepping stones that take me closer and closer to God.

Confession 19

DID SHE REALLY JUST ASK THAT?! (PART 2)

AT SUMMER CAMP ONE YEAR, all the high school girls and their counselors took half a morning for girl talk. One of the stories that came out was about a young man who was struggling in life and faith, and the young woman in whom he confided. She thought this deep emotional intimacy would lead to a romantic relationship, but it had the opposite effect, to the point where they were no longer even friends. Why?

Emotional Virginity

Many girls are used to being emotionally intimate with their friends, even their guy friends, their sisters, their mom, and so on. That's what girl talk is, right? Girls talk about how they feel at the drop of a hat. But most boys do not, and emotional intimacy is largely new territory.

In this story, the young man bared everything he had before the relationship was mature. He jumped right into intimacy, and it destroyed the relationship. (Mentally, compare this to having physical relations with someone after two dates.) Maybe it is shame or frustration with yourself. Maybe it is anger at the other person for pushing too hard or a desire to pretend it never happened. But rarely does a relationship survive this leap into intimacy.

Emotional intimacy grows with time and conversation. There are things about you no one else knows. Secrets you have never told anyone. In many ways all people have an unquenchable thirst to be understood and accepted because God created us for Himself, and He knows us fully without exception. This desire (or lust) to be known can lead to oversharing in any relationship. Revealing one's heart is an aspect of love that is often overlooked and, like intellectual virginity, taken for granted.

Intellectual Virginity

During my clinical year of physician assistant school, I had a Muslim preceptor. We were both deep thinkers who operated from a faith background, and since he had abandoned his religion, he found my orthodox faith even more intriguing. He enjoyed the verbal sparring and testing of wits. We spent hours beyond the typical workday discussing God, faith, and the Bible. I distinctly remember telling my mother it was like he was having an affair with my mind. That time, energy, depth of discussion, and privilege of seeing how he thought and reasoned should have belonged to his wife.

Intellectual virginity can be clustered under emotional virginity. But whereas emotional virginity centers around expressing one's feelings, intellectual virginity is about sharing how one thinks about the world. This kind of intimacy is an aspect of a close and complex relationship. It extends beyond the facts to understanding how an individual processes and responds to that information.

This is how an older couple can go out to dinner and he can order exactly what she wants while she is in the restroom. If you asked him how he knew what to order, he might say something like this: "Well, I knew normally she would like the fish. But it's raining, and chicken always reminds her of a home-cooked meal in a warm kitchen. So I ordered her chicken and dumplings with a green salad because I know she is on a health kick, and it would make her feel better about the chocolate lava cake we are going to split for dessert . . . Even though I actually ordered it for me, I know she will want some."

He knows her, main course to dessert, because they have been intellectually intimate for forty years.

This kind of intimacy is the result of investing time and effort simply because you love someone. Everyone we meet knows us to some degree. Our parents and siblings, generally, know us well. Our close friends know us pretty well. Intellectual virginity, like emotional virginity, isn't about concealing ourselves but about moving at a wise pace in our relationships.

The emotional virgin . . . wait . . . that didn't come out right at all. I am trying to convey the concept of safeguarding your romantic love for your husband. I am not trying to say that being a virgin makes you emotionally unstable or that that would be desirable. Ah . . . the English language.

In English we may correctly say, I love my dog, I love hot dogs, and I love my husband. Grammatically they are all correct, but we understand I would give up hot dogs for my dog, and I would give up hot dogs and even my dog for my spouse. The word is the same, but the intensity is worlds apart.

When we talk about emotional and intellectual intimacy, we mean saving our love (as in, I love my spouse) for marriage; or, as Solomon put it, guarding your heart (Proverbs 4:23). Guarding your heart can be thought of simply and inclusively. It is saving my "I love you" (romantically speaking) for one person and one person only. This extends to the actual words and the related actions and thoughts— even ones others may see as fully innocent.

Emotional virginity is harder to guard than physical virginity. It involves boundless trust and openness, sharing hopes and dreams, failures and fears. This interaction between a couple is more profound than friendship and at a deeper level than even your relationships with your siblings or parents. For a single in the church, setting emotional and intellectual boundaries is an important skill. Too distant or superficial and we can't get to know each other at any meaningful level. But jump in too quickly and an immature relationship will likely implode under the weight. Too deeply, especially with married men, and we can steal from their wives this special privilege of knowing them.

Relationships are like cooking. It's an art based on a science. A recent devotion from *First15* noted, "We were not created to offer our affections to anyone or anything but God first and foremost."[1] This is the science portion of relationships. There is no substitute for intentionally spending quality time with God. If we ignore this foundational truth, we shouldn't be surprised if our friendships fizzle and fade with time. But if we choose to love God first, He will bring wisdom and balance to our relationships—romantic and otherwise.

One of the ways we can choose to love God first (rather than marriage or another person) is to purposefully meditate on God's Word and refuse to habitually daydream about the perfect mate or a particular person. This not only reserves our intellect for God's use but keeps our emotions grounded in the truth. Now we are prepared to move forward.

The opportunity to get to know someone is a gift to be respected and treasured. Be patient, and avoid the temptation to make that relationship the center of your life. Continuing to nurture your other relationships with friends, family, and God will protect you from pressuring your new relationship before it is mature.

In a relationship, information is like salt—you can always add more. This is the art of relationships. Try discussing only what you both are comfortable with and avoiding conversations about the future. During the early stages of a relationship, this can help you focus on getting to know each other and avoid pushing the relationship too quickly. It can also be useful to identify which circumstances make you more likely to overshare, like drinking alcohol (which can be dangerous on multiple levels), or talking late at night or after a romantic movie or event. Knowing what these circumstances are for you might prompt you to avoid them, limit them, or change them (like by inviting others to join you).

Spiritual Virginity

If you are ever in Farmington, New Mexico, during the week before Easter, I recommend attending the *Passion Play*. This play is a reenactment of Christ's passion week, starting with His triumphal entry into Jerusalem and culminating at the resurrection. Hundreds of people from dozens of churches partner together to reach their community with the gospel of Jesus Christ. The first time I was in the play, I showed up for tryouts, only to spend the first half hour as a cast member in worship and prayer.

Standing together with the cast and crew, I heard Christ's modern-day disciples, from a half dozen denominations, entreat the God of the universe. It was a startlingly intimate experience.

Physical virginity is about reserving your sight and touch for your husband's body.

Emotional virginity is about the singular privilege of understanding your husband's feelings and vice versa.

Intellectual virginity is about your husband knowing how you think and you knowing how he thinks better than anyone else.

But spiritual virginity is about joining in your husband's relationship with God—an exclusive relationship for man and wife and their Creator.

Never will you have a clearer portrait of someone than when you pray together, listen to each other's insights into God's Word, or see your spouse worship when they think they are alone. Spiritual virginity is easy to keep because most people do not even realize it exists. And many never enter into spiritual intimacy at all, not even within marriage.

> People speak all the time of a couple being joined at the hip, but a couple who shares a relationship with God is joined at the soul.

Those we go to church or Bible study with see part of us that is very personal. But even they see only a sliver of our faith. It is our husbands who will see us praying, studying Scripture, dissecting theology, teaching our children how to love God, and worshipping our Lord in an apron and bare feet. But—and this is why Paul spoke so emphatically about not marrying an unbeliever (2 Corinthians 6:14)—it is not enough to witness our walk with Jesus. Marriage is designed for husband and wife to walk with Jesus together.

People speak all the time of a couple being joined at the hip, but a couple who shares a relationship with God is joined at the soul. True spiritual intimacy is found only in marriage, as the only shared relationship with God.

Perhaps you have read about the three-strand cord in Ecclesiastes 4:12. Perhaps, like most, you think it just happens like magic. But it doesn't. Those three strands are woven together by pursuing God as a couple. Studying and meditating on God's Word together. Ministering and praying alongside each other. Praying separately (including for each other) and coming together again (1 Corinthians 7:5). When a husband and wife seek the presence of God as a unit, they are inviting the Lord into the heart of their marriage.

According to bridal writer Lana Vrz, "God's purpose for the marriage relationship is to be the door of the Christian home. The loving relationship between wife and husband should give the clearest blueprint of Christ's love. The representation . . . would genuinely draw others to the love of Christ."[2] When a couple adopts God's vision for their relationship, home, and ministry, they are obeying the directives of the One who created marriage. He is where the strength for marriage comes from. You cannot help but be emotionally and intellectually intertwined while sharing openly about and seeking answers from God.

Virginity is God's design for singleness. Physical. Emotional. Intellectual. Spiritual. And total intimacy in these areas is God's design for marriage.

In football, there's one team made up of offense and defense. The offense doesn't do what the defense does and vice versa, but they encourage each other and both benefit when the other does their job well.

There is one church made up of single and married people. As we fulfill God's design for us to be holy in body and soul (1 Corinthians 7:34), we are in the position to be cheerleaders for the marriages around us. We know the loneliness and longing we deal with, and we can remind our sisters and brothers to cherish each other and enjoy the blessings of marriage. As they fulfill God's design for intimacy (1 Corinthians 7:3), they are in a position to encourage us in purity. They know the struggles and the questions they dealt with before marriage, and they can urge us to be diligent in our undistracted faith and service.

It's almost as if God knew that the differences in our lives would enable us to support each other . . . like a family . . . the family of God.

—— REFLECT ——

With God, healthy and balanced relationships are possible. How can you be sincere and transparent without oversharing or being self-centered? How do wise habits build strong relationships and protect others, especially married men?

—— PRAY ——

Talk to God about being single in a community of couples. Pray for the married couples in your life.

—— TAKE A SINGLE STEP ——

Even the word *virgin* evokes an image of loneliness. Choose one verse, like Psalm 84:11, Psalm 113:9, or Galatians 4:27, and memorize it for when loneliness is winning. One of my favorites is Isaiah 56:3–5:

Do not let the son of the foreigner
Who has joined himself to the LORD
Speak, saying,
"The LORD has utterly separated me from His people";
Nor let the eunuch say,
"Here I am, a dry tree."
For thus says the LORD:
"To the eunuchs who keep My Sabbaths,
And choose what pleases Me,
And hold fast My covenant,
Even to them I will give in My house
And within My walls a place and a name
Better than that of sons and daughters;
I will give them an everlasting name
That shall not be cut off."

How often have we felt dry and useless? Which of us hasn't looked at our friend's children and thought, *God has left me empty*? But then God reaches down and hugs us. He has given us a place in His house and His family. The Lord has made our future secure and fruitful.

Confession 20

A DIFFERENT QUESTION

DUTCHESS WAS A QUIRKY BLACK dog with plenty of life experience. Rez (shorthand for Native American Reservation) dogs are like that. They come from hardy, muddled stock, and many have sad stories. Dutchess did.

She was abandoned at a construction site on a nearby reservation, probably because she was pregnant. By the time we met, she was scared of everything, heavily pregnant, and limping due to a dog-fight. Soon after she moved in, she mothered eight puppies. The puppies grew and went to new homes, and though we thought it would go away, her limp remained. And after ten years, all that time spent limping did something I didn't foresee. Her abnormal gait suddenly began causing her terrible pain, for which the vet had no answers.

You see, even though everyone who'd ever seen her knew about Dutchess's limp, it didn't seem like a big deal. None of us realized her reluctance to use her leg normally would irreparably damage her spine and incapacitate her. The truth was her leg had healed and she didn't need to limp anymore, but the habit of hopping around eventually crippled her completely.

I have a limp in my life that would do the same thing to me . . . if

I let it. You and I might even have the same limp. But limps notwithstanding, I have a riddle for you: What do a Christian spinster, an out-of-work plumber, and a cancer patient have in common?

If anything jumps to mind, hold those thoughts and consider part of the story of Abraham. For eighty years his limp was the fact that he had no heir, which in his culture was as good as being dead. Abraham had many moments of superhuman faith, but perhaps none more than his willingness to sacrifice his miraculous only son and heir. I find it thought provoking that this particular story comes nearer to the end of the patriarch's life.

Hebrews 11:19 tells us Abraham had concluded God was able to raise Isaac up—even if he was dead—to accomplish His plans and fulfill His promises. This had never happened before. No one before Abraham had been brought back from the dead. But in his unwavering faith, Abraham reasoned that God could reverse death. He was correct.

A Christian spinster, an out-of-work plumber, and a cancer patient all have the opportunity to answer the question Abraham found himself facing thousands of years ago. Is God enough? Is He enough if my only son is dead? If I will be alone forever, is Jesus enough? What if the bank account is empty or my body fails me?

We sing quite a few songs that say "Christ is enough." I dislike it when the lyricist tacks on "for me," because it alters the focus and meaning of the statement. I choose to believe this is a personal testimony to a timeless truth. But it is important that this is a universal truth about God, because in the turmoil of our lives, the temptation is already to turn inward, toward me, instead of upward, toward God.

"Is God enough for me?" is a much different question than "Is God enough?" In the first, the focus slips from God, who has proved Himself more than enough throughout all of human history, to me, whose perception is flawed and stunted. From my perspective, I may not be able to tell if God is enough. But if I step back and answer the question "Is God enough?" I can confidently assert the truth: God is enough. Period.

He was enough for Abraham even if Isaac was dead. He is enough for the cancer patient even if physical health is stripped away. He is enough for the plumber who is financially broke. And He is enough for the Christian spinster who faces a future alone.

Christ is sufficient.

When we believe lies about singleness, we fool ourselves into believing that

$$God + Marriage = Enough$$

Instead of believing the truth, which is that

$$God = Always Enough$$

This fact is easily buried in the beauty of family. But some of us get a chance to prove it with the evidence of our lives in singleness.

Being a living example of God's all-sufficiency can be painful. It can be confusing. It can be twisted for selfish gain. It may even be enough to cause a Dutchess limp—a wound that we refuse to receive healing for.

If we cling to our limp, we will never be sure God is enough. But if we put weight on it, faith in God's all-sufficiency yields a joy-filled life that brings peace, healing, and songs in the night (Job 35:10). It is a peace that passes understanding through the longest winters and most intense storms (Philippians 4:7). It is a healing that is possible because God stands as our rear guard (Isaiah 58:8). This life built on Jesus, the rock of our salvation, is forever secure (2 Samuel 22:47).

Whether we get married or not. Whether we have children or not. Whether we get the future we think we want or not . . . God is enough, and we are assured that He will vindicate His children. We need not be or live embarrassed of our calling or godly choices.

Our culture wants Christians to be ashamed of God and the sacrifices we make to obey God. They want to disgrace those of us who serve God instead of self. They want to shame us for striving for purity in our relationships. Our society pounces on Christian singles and would rip us apart as foolish and naive. They mock those of us who possess their bodily vessels with honor as fitting a child of God (2 Timothy 2:21) and, paradoxically, mercilessly ridicule us if we fail. The world cannot be satisfied. It is time to stop limping and walk on. We have a choice to be ashamed or not.

As Adam and Eve demonstrated, shame follows sin. And being ashamed of our wrong thoughts, wrong beliefs, and wrongdoings is appropriate (Daniel 9:8). But when we confess and forsake our sins, in Jesus Christ we stand fully forgiven and free from our past mistakes, and there is no reason to continue in shame. Even if others do not understand them, God's standards are good and true, and there is no reason to be embarrassed. We are promised that what is right will be evident in the last day, and those who have chosen these things are wise and "shall shine," vindicated "forever and ever" (Daniel 12:2–3).

Christian singles are in a unique position to live fully unashamed, to live out the reality that God is enough, and to construct a beacon of hope with our lives. Our lives scream, "WE HOPE IN GOD ALONE." We are not slaves to our sexual desires or our emotions. We are not tied to the triviality of our world or to the fickleness of our culture. We do not have to spend our lives searching for fulfillment, because the presence of God is life, fullness of joy, and pleasures forever (Psalm 16:11).

The world can mock our chastity. God is right.

It can belittle our choices to guard our hearts, but God is still right.

As singles we have the opportunity to spend our lives lavishly on Christ.

It can deride our archaic adherence to Christ, but God will be shown right.

As singles we have the opportunity to spend our lives lavishly on Christ. Let the world watch. We can choose to live in confident defiance of societal norms because they are wrong and God is right. In our loneliness, our holiness, our selflessness, we declare we were made for God and He is enough.

We don't need to limp.

REFLECT

How is God offering you healing? Consider things like past mistakes, unfulfilled dreams, and damaged relationships. How has He comforted you? How has He worked through those situations? And how may those painful experiences equip you to comfort and encourage others?

PRAY

Ask God to show you where you are limping. Where do you need to receive the healing He is holding out to you?

TAKE A SINGLE STEP

Fill in the following sentence, and write it on a sticky note: Today I ask for and receive healing for _____.

Post your note on your bathroom mirror, your refrigerator, or somewhere you will see it multiple times today. Each time you read that note, remind yourself: God has provided me healing.

Confession 21

THE SILLY, SCARY, AND SOUND—
ADVICE ON GETTING MARRIED

PEOPLE IN GENERAL HAVE ALWAYS been free with their advice to unmarried women. During the 1800s, the general advice, such as that from *Collier's Encyclopedia of Social and Commercial Information* or *The Young Wife* by William Andrus Alcott published in 1837, was along the lines of the following: Look pretty, smile, and be demure. Don't talk too much or too loudly. And for heaven's sake, don't talk about science or politics or international relations or business. (Which, of course, begs the question: What should women talk about?)

Clearly somewhat silly advice.

Starting in the 1900s, the advice, mostly gleaned from entertainment, got more racy and less helpful. Date as much as you can. Physically, feel free to do whatever you want—just don't get emotionally involved. And for heaven's sake, make sure you are in control and he knows it. (Which is, of course, the foundation for a loving, lasting marriage . . . uh, no.)

Clearly excellent advice for divorce, poor self-esteem, and abject disaster. I have gotten a fair amount of advice on "getting married" (but very little on being single, which is interesting). Honestly, for the most part, the advice I have been given falls on a scale from silly to scary to sound.

The Silly: Be More Attractive

Quick! What is the most ridiculous advice you've ever gotten? I'm sure we've all heard our fair share. Starting around age thirteen, I heard from various people that I should wear more makeup. (Incidentally, this is in direct contradiction to the Victorian-era wisdom on womanhood.) I distinctly remember a speech judge in high school making a point that I should wear mascara. "Otherwise, your eyes seem to sink into your head," she said.

Even to my high school brain that sounded petty. I couldn't understand. *I like me. Why don't you like me? And if you don't like me, is making this change really going to change your opinion?* Not only did wearing mascara seem unnecessary, but it also seemed to reflect misplaced time and priorities. *And further,* I reasoned, *how much should I want to change your perception of me?*

Wearing mascara was an issue for me because redheads are about one step away from albino, and black mascara over clear eyelashes is a startling look but not an attractive one. Where I grew up, 90-plus percent of the population was Navajo, rendering anything other than black mascara obscure and difficult to come by. (Yes, I know I am dating myself.)

> Beauty is evidence of God's touch, and our beauty pleases God.

So my final decision was no. Not only did I have no way of procuring appropriate mascara, but, I decided, makeup or not wouldn't really change what others thought of me. It would only change what they thought of the outside of me, and that kind of pretty was fleeting.

All of us get to make similar choices about our beauty: our shoes, our clothes, our nails, our faces. But in the end, it is God who makes all things beautiful in His time (Ecclesiastes 3:11).

Beauty is evidence of God's touch, and our beauty pleases God (Psalm 45:11). We think of beauty as largely appealing to our sense of sight. But it is available to all our senses.

Our ears hear beauty in music, the sounds of nature, and the voices of our families and friends. And God is working in us to make what we say pure, true, and encouraging. He is making our voices beautiful.

We feel beauty in dance and in strength as our bodies fulfill what they were created to do. And God is sustaining our bodies to serve and uphold others. He is making our feet and our hands beautiful.

We taste and smell beauty in food. We crave spicy, sweet, and savory flavors. And day by day the Author of beauty is sculpting us into a sweet-smelling sacrifice to Himself—one that brings Him glory and pleasure (2 Corinthians 2:14–15).

And in case you are wondering, I still don't wear mascara except on special occasions.

The Scary: Lower Your Standards

"You need to be less picky." This was the recommendation of a friend from church. And I really believe she thinks she gave me good advice. And she did, if the sole purpose of life is to get married.

But I have a confession (and I really hope you hear me on this one): marriage is not the goal of life. And yet maybe you have heard these— or similar—pieces of helpful advice from well-meaning people:

"Bring your skirt up a few inches (or maybe a foot), and believe me, more guys will be interested." True, but what kind of men find this attractive?

"Date everyone who asks—that way men will know you're available." (Stop laughing—I have actually been told this.)

"Allow more physical contact—you'll keep your boyfriend."

"So what if a man doesn't want to provide for you or a family. That's so old-fashioned anyway. Just let it go. He's going to church with you; he doesn't really have to be a Christian, does he? Stop being so exacting."

"Lower your standards" is crazy, antibiblical advice. It is a quick fix to a nonexistent problem at the cost of a lifetime of frustration and regret because either you get married using this advice or you get used. In the first you are stuck for life, and in the second you are injured for life. And either way we have disobeyed God:

> But you, O man of God, flee these things and pursue righteousness, godliness, faith, love, patience, gentleness. (1 Timothy 6:11)

The Sound: It Would Be a Waste

If you don't have a brother, you don't understand how humbling it is when your brother is right. Especially when he's younger than you.

It is, and was, no secret in our family that I want to be married. One day, many years ago now, my brother and I were discussing it (which proves what a good brother I have), and this is what he said: "I think it would be a waste for you." End of conversation.

I was irritated. He thought *my* dreams for *my* life would be a waste of *my* time and talents. *What an arrogant thing for anyone to think*, I reasoned in my head, *that I am too good for marriage.*

I blew it off. Or tried to, but I couldn't forget.

Because he was right. Not that I am extraordinary, but because it is always a waste for any of us to do anything other than what God has called us to do.

This fact should not paralyze us into inaction (see "Confession 24: A Fairy-Tale Ending"), but rather motivate us to live out God's individual calling for us as His singles. This is the time to deepen our relationship with God, to practice obedience, and to be devoted in our service. Our single years allow us time and flexibility to grow in character and become more and more like Jesus in our words, thoughts, and actions.

The Eldredges say in *Captivating*, "You have only one life to live. It would be best to live your own"[1]—and this is also what Paul was saying to the Corinthians. Paraphrased, 1 Corinthians 7:27 says, "Are you single? Don't seek to be married. Are you married? Don't seek to be single. Serve God the way He has called you to serve— don't waste time wishing you had someone else's calling."

It is a calling to be single. To refuse that calling would be to waste God's gift.

REFLECT

What was your knee-jerk reaction to my brother's comment about marriage being a waste for me? If something is wasted, it is not used properly. Have you been wasting God's calling of singleness? If you have, confess it to God and move forward. What is one practical change you can make today to use your singleness more effectively?

PRAY

Each of the following passages discusses God's will. Pray through at least one of these, and commit to fulfilling God's calling for you that is revealed in them.

Ephesians 6:5–8—working for the Lord and not people

1 Thessalonians 4:3–8—maintaining sexual holiness

1 Corinthians 6:15–20—possessing ourselves with honor

Hebrews 10:35–39—enduring to the end

1 Peter 2:13–17—living the example in our communities

1 John 2:15–17—abiding in the Lord while living in the world

———— TAKE A SINGLE STEP ————

How can you ensure your encouragement and counsel to others is sound, not silly or scary? Try answering the questions you have asked others over the years. Is your advice consistent with God's Word? Is it something you would have been able to accept when you were the one asking the questions?

Confession 22

THE "M" WORD AND A FEW FRIENDS

GROWING UP ON THE NAVAJO Reservation made for many unique experiences, not the least of which were the long Saturday afternoons spent exploring on dirt roads. My best friend's brother had an ancient, two-wheel-drive, bright-yellow truck. Through much trial and error, he convinced his little truck it was a four-wheel-drive beast, able to traverse anything from sand to snow.

This particular Saturday we found what appeared to be a dry lake bed in the mountains. The vehicle I was riding in skirted the area because there was a conspicuous absence of tire tracks within the lake basin. But the battle-hardened canary on wheels scorned the safety of the edge and zipped across the basin floor.

Then, BOOM!

The truck's rear wheels were buried past the axles. The speed had not been enough to overcome the sinkhole. It wasn't just muddy; it was the consistency of setting concrete, and it was deep.

The rest of the afternoon we learned and utilized a practical life skill that has since served me well: getting unstuck. But as challenging as getting a one-ton truck out of the mud is, there are many things in life much harder to extricate yourself from.

Three times in thirty years, that is how often I have heard masturbation addressed in any Christian forum. I read about it once in a book—for men.[1] I heard it once in a sermon—for men—by pastor and theologian John Piper and once at camp during a talk for teenage girls. We just don't talk about the "M" word in Christian circles (and we rarely seriously address pornography or other personal sexual sins).

Honestly, I'd rather not talk about secret sexual sins. It's uncomfortable and embarrassing, and . . . well, you get the idea. But the truth is this: if Christians do not hear about these sinkholes from mature Christ-followers, they will learn about them some other way, possibly with devastating consequences.

In football, the quarterback has a guard dedicated to protecting his back, his blind side. It is bad enough to be slammed into the turf if you see it coming. But when you don't see it coming, it can cost you the game or even end your career. Speaking from experience, discovering masturbation (or pornography) with no foreknowledge or insight is like being blindsided by an NFL linebacker.

So let's get real.

"Masturbation is a sin," the camp speaker said. That was it. No explanation or biblical reasoning.

When there is no context for a topic such as masturbation, it leaves us confused and curious.

I remember sitting in the audience thinking, *That's not a good answer for anyone.* The younger ladies in attendance likely did not know that masturbation is sexually stimulating oneself. So the speaker's answer was downright dangerous because they now had questions that (God forbid) they'd ask the internet. For years this was the way pornography was discussed in church: with an appropriate sense of shame but without a definition. So as a ten- or twelve-year-old, I knew pornography was embarrassing (so you couldn't ask about it) and sinful (thank God the internet was in its infancy), but I didn't know what it was, which was not helpful.

But the speaker's comment on masturbation was also so shallow that for those women who had already fallen into this sinkhole, it didn't seem likely his advice would help them climb out. Not even close. Tasting that kind of gratification through a sexual indulgence, especially when no one else knows, is addictive. Each individual has to decide if they should even want to get out. After all, it is easy to justify: "I'm not hurting anyone, and this may be all I ever get." (This is essentially the same excuse given for all sexual sins.) As Christians, we know some things are wrong. Don't lie. Don't steal. Don't murder. Those are easy. But some things the Bible does not clearly label as sin: alcohol, smoking, drugs, entertainment, and so on. Now we have to make a judgment call, and that's harder than simply saying "absolutely not."

On the face of it, the Bible doesn't address masturbation or pornography. Any Christian kid knows it's wrong to have sex with someone else if you aren't married. But this isn't someone else, is it? The Bible doesn't say it's wrong. And as a young woman, since no one ever told me about it, who was I going to ask? Certainly not Google (at least I had that much sense).

Let me be clear. Most people think masturbation and pornography are purely male dilemmas. They aren't. They affect the sexes differently but no less damagingly.[2]

For years any mention of pornography perked up my ears as I tried to figure out what it was. During a sermon a pastor told a story that finally defined pornography as inappropriate pictures of people performing sexual acts. In my young mind, I wondered, *Why didn't you just say that to begin with?!*

Masturbation was mentioned so infrequently I didn't figure it out in church. I figured it out in a classroom, which is not ideal, but at least I knew what it was when I came across it in Christian circles. Both the book I read and the sermon I heard said basically the same thing: never start masturbating, because it leads to sins like pornography, adultery, fornication, or lasciviousness. And this is true. Why else would Solomon say not to walk by her house (Proverbs 5:8) or imagine going there (Proverbs 7:25)? Obviously, these things are a temptation to sin.

But if you are already addicted and it doesn't match your experience, this argument is very difficult to accept. It's hard to believe that what satisfies you now will cease to do so in the future, even though this is the addictive pattern, be it sex, drugs, or alcohol. Most of us think, *I have this vice under control. It's like a sober woman having a beer, not an alcoholic drinking a pint of vodka.*

So why should we avoid masturbation and pornography and the like? Because a speaker says it's wrong? Or an author says it will lead to worse sin?

As I looked around this camp chapel filled with women thirteen to fifty-three, I thought, *We need more. Please, give us more.*

I had one place left to go: the Bible and its Author. God does not individually address every topic in His Word. But I am convinced He does establish principles to address every topic.

When Paul said, "All things are lawful for me, but not all things are helpful; all things are lawful for me, but not all things edify" (1 Corinthians 10:23), he was specifically teaching about eating meat offered to idols. But the principle pertains to any area where the Bible is vague.

This premise is expanded on in Romans 14, where Paul is teaching about "doubtful things" and Christian freedom. Here Paul lays out guidelines for how we are to use our freedom (one of our gifts as singles!).

We are God's. Our freedom is from and for Him (Romans 14:7–8). All of us who have committed our lives to Christ cannot dispute this on any level. He is God. He deserves all worship and full loyalty. We shall have no other gods before Him (Exodus 20:3). If anything takes His place, distracts from His worship, or demands what belongs to Him, it is certainly sin (Exodus 34:14). Even if it is something good, like ministry, career, or family, it is still sin to serve it.

We are to put others first and duly consider how our choices impact them (Romans 14:15–19). If my freedom is influencing another to sin, I am wrong. If my choices are hurting someone else, I am sinning. In connection with masturbation (include pornography and sexual daydreams), how would this affect my spouse? Is it stealing from them what is rightfully theirs?

My conclusion was that this habit feeds self-centeredness, which is unloving and unfair to my future husband. Beyond that, it is stealing from him a gift God created for him to give to me: sexual satisfaction. If I am satisfied with masturbation or pornography or voyeurism (or fill in the blank), how can I be the sexual partner God has created me to be?

We are called to live by faith with a clear conscience toward God and in right relationship with others (Romans 14:19). When we live free from sin, we are living by faith because whatever is not from faith is sin (verse 23). When we choose to obey God's commands, we are refusing to be controlled by the dictates of our own hearts. We are trusting His grace when we fail, but not abusing that grace to satisfy our self-absorbed desires.

> And do this, knowing the time, that now it is high time to awake out of sleep; for now our salvation is nearer than when we first believed. The night is far spent, the day is at hand. Therefore let us cast off the works of darkness, and let us put on the armor of light. Let us walk properly, as in the day, not in revelry and drunkenness, not in lewdness and lust, not in strife and envy. But put on the Lord Jesus Christ, and make no provision for the flesh, to fulfill its lusts. (Romans 13:11–14)

Anyone can justify any behavior if they want to badly enough. But as God's daughters, sin no longer has dominion over us (Romans

6:14); we can rule over it (Genesis 4:7). But if we allow lust in any form to become a recurring and intrusive theme in our thoughts, it distracts us from everything, most importantly our pursuit of God, and as Piper says, it "stands in the way of obedience."[3] An addiction of any kind is a competitor for God's place in our lives—an idol has usurped Christ's throne. Now we need God's help (2 Samuel 22:18). Our enemy has been unveiled, and we understand this battle is too much for us. But when we repent, our past mistakes are no longer held against us, and God hears our cries for aid. He does not leave us shut up in the hand of our Enemy but instead sets our feet in a wide place (Psalm 31:8).

Because even though we foolishly fall prey to these vicious enemies, our Lord is fully prepared and always leads us in triumph in Christ (2 Corinthians 2:14). And though we stumble and fall, no sin has the right to rule over us because we live under the grace of our Savior. Christ knows every single one of our sins and still stands before God advocating for us (1 John 2:1). So if we fail today, we will get up and try again tomorrow because Jesus will still be standing there urging us on.

> Simple, purposeful tactics and habits can protect us from our old selves and provide us the way of escape.

Now is the time to find and map ways out of sexual sinkholes. Many of these ways out are straightforward, practical changes to defend yourself. Consider strategies like these:

- Finding a mentor for accountability and encouragement.
- Meeting with a Christian counselor for godly insight and support.

- Installing a filter on your computer. (This protects everyone who uses it—not just you.)
- Using an accountability app.
- Ensuring you are tired when you go to bed so your mind has less opportunity to wander.
- Singing or meditating on Scripture as you go to sleep.
- Fleeing temptation, whether that means turning off the TV, computer, or smart device, turning on the light, or calling someone.

Simple, purposeful tactics and habits can protect us from our old selves and provide us the way of escape. Father, let our hearts always be determined to worship and serve You alone.

REFLECT

Spend some time alone in God's presence seeking His face and seeking wisdom to pursue chastity.

PRAY

Praise God that He protects us from sin and gives us victory over it. Ask Him to help you guard your thoughts as you seek to put Him first in all areas of your life.

TAKE A SINGLE STEP

Implement one tactic to protect yourself from secret sexual sins.

Confession 23

THE OTHER "M" WORD

I AM A PHYSICIAN ASSISTANT. Years ago, when I was still in school, I was in physical exam class, where we were learning how to do a shoulder exam. Our professor asked one of the male students to take off his shirt so we could see the "landmarks" (anatomical structures that help a medical professional do an exam or procedure).

(You may be thinking, *That is inappropriate*, but it is not uncommon for any kind of medical training to use students for demonstrations.)

It just so happened that this particular gentleman was in excellent physical condition. A point that the ladies in the class quickly keyed in on with giggles and several sexually appreciative remarks.

He looked embarrassed, and I felt embarrassed for him. Our reaction moved him from being our classmate—who was fun and studied hard—to being an object to us.

In his article "Battling the Unbelief of Lust," Piper says, "Lust is a sexual desire that dishonors its object and disregards God. It's the corruption of a good thing by the absence of honorable commitment and by the absence of a supreme regard for God."[1] When we lust after someone else, our view of them changes. They become an object that can potentially fulfill our sexual fantasies. This is true across the board, whether the person is physically with you, as in adultery and fornication, or not, as in sexting or pornography.

Lust is a lie. Because I am not just a sexual being and neither are you.

As author Dr. Craig von Buseck says, "Man is made up of physical material, the body, that can be seen and touched. But he is also made up of immaterial aspects, which are intangible—this includes the soul, spirit, intellect, will, emotions, conscience, and so forth."[2] And each part of us influences our whole being. Physical input, for example, influences the mind. The state of our mind informs our emotional and spiritual health.

We were at a missions conference once when several people mentioned how vastly women outnumber men on the mission field. A staff member from the mission board raised a hand. "Can I say something? I just really want to speak to this issue of men in the mission field."

The president nodded. The ambassador from the mission board said, "There's a reason that women outnumber men."

I imagine we all expected to hear something about the lack of Christian men, or that men are unwilling or not applying, or that they are distracted by making money or promoting their careers. But that's not what she said.

"The reason is pornography." It took guts to say that to this audience of senior church ladies, pastors, and ministry workers. "They are disqualified because of addictions to pornography." My spirit sank as I thought over and over, *We need to fight harder for our men.*

What she said made sense. I knew porn had touched my family. The Barna Group reported in 2014 that 64 percent of Christian men and 15 percent of Christian women use pornography monthly.[3] And in 2016, surveys showed 20 percent of youth pastors and 14 percent of lead pastors regularly view pornography, while 43 percent of pastors had struggled with it in the past.[4] We are a family—we are God's family. Their failures (like ours) not only affect all of us, but they represent part of our responsibility to bear one another's burdens (Galatians 6:2). It's a command.

Satan is picking off our men, and we women need to fight for and support and encourage them to walk worthy of the calling God has placed on their lives.

Proverbs 7:6–27 is the story of a foolish young man's rendezvous with an unfaithful woman. He's hanging around the wrong place at the wrong time. She's dressed in all the wrong ways and says all the wrong things. He doesn't know it, but it's going to cost him his life. Many men much savvier than he are already dead at her feet.

It's tempting to read this chapter and pass over it. I invite you to resist that temptation. This woman is not a harlot (verse 10). She is an embodiment of all forms of sexual temptation, and they all lead to the same place—hell (verse 27).

Yes, this man was careless. Yes, he failed to exercise self-control. He was fully responsible for allowing her to seduce him. But in Solomon's story, the young man is alone. What if instead a sister had called him back? "That's not wise—this is a bad place to be." Her voice and presence may have been enough to sway him to continue on the straight and narrow path.

So how do we become those wise sisters?

First, we minister in light of the grace God has given to us as singles (1 Peter 4:10). We accept the reality that sexual temptation exists, and this will limit how we fight.

My sister and brother-in-law have a pact. If anyone breaks into their house, my brother-in-law goes for the gun and my sister goes for their son. They are both protecting, just in different ways.

As we step into the battle to protect our brothers and sisters from sexual sins, our protection will look different, depending on the person. We must establish appropriate boundaries as we minister. We may not offer to be accountability partners for men, like we might for women. We may only go out to coffee for one-on-one prayer time with other ladies, but we will be faithfully interceding for both sexes.

Second, we pray. Prayer invites the Holy Spirit into the fray. Conversation with Him not only keeps our thoughts toward our brothers and sisters pure, but it allows us to fight their battles alongside them. Philippians 1:9–11 and Colossians 1:9–11 are both prayers for the churches.

I have unashamedly plagiarized these prayers many times because I can't do better than the Holy Spirit. Whether you are male or female, Paul's prayers are always appropriate and needful. We must start this conflict on our knees because we are wrestling against powers of the darkness of this age (Ephesians 6:12). If we fight apart from God, we will surely lose.

Third, we grow in our role as sisters as we understand our role as servants. A servant's first goal is the will of her master. As servants of Christ, our first priority is Him. As we put on Christ's character, we are enabled to serve others patiently and humbly in love (Colossians 3:12–14).

For married brothers and sisters, this can be as simple as asking how their spouse is when only one is at church or praising their spouse to them. For all brothers and sisters, putting them first may look like hospitality, helping them in ministry, consistently praying for them (and remembering to ask them about their prayer requests and how God has been answering), and so on. Remember: we are family.

As Christ's Word dwells in us richly, it transforms us and empowers us to teach, offer wise counsel, and give needful correction (Colossians 3:16). We are to encourage all, but especially those less mature than ourselves, to shun secret sexual sins. We may serve them best by continuing in prayer and suggesting or introducing them to a godly mentor, such as a pastor, a deacon or deaconess, or a licensed counselor.

Fourth, as wise sisters, we need to take heed to how our words, attitudes, and actions influence others. It only takes one student to distract the class—every teacher knows this, and so does every camp counselor (or camp nurse, in my case).

"But how are we going to measure?" one of the female camp counselors asked.

"What about fingertip length?" someone suggested.

"But some people have really long arms."

"Or short arms."

"What about three inches above the knee?"

I zoned out. It's not like the camp nurse needs to get involved in determining the acceptable length of shorts. And while I do vigilantly support wearing closed-toe shoes for all athletic activities, this protracted debate was bringing back childhood memories of receiving dress codes that were multiple pages long.

I've been to three camp counselors' meetings. Would you like to know a secret? We spend more time discussing the dress code than anything else (even food). And it isn't just shorts. What about swimsuits? If they are two piece, but they overlap in the middle, is that okay? (The camp's requirement that every swimmer wear a dark T-shirt silenced this debate.) How tight can jeans be? What about rips? Shirts need sleeves, but what constitutes a sleeve?

Why do we even have to have these meetings? What is the problem? The basic problem is sin. Sin has reduced the human body to an object of lust. And until we are sinless, we need help keeping our hearts and minds pure, and we need to help others do the same. We call this modesty.

The classic definition of what is modest has to do with how tight, long, and thick a woman's clothes are. And the typical consensus is men don't have to worry about it . . . until they have teenage daughters. Only women, especially if they are single, need to worry about modesty. And especially if they are skinny and/or not skinny in the right places.

That is the general but inaccurate view of modesty, in my opinion.

Modesty applies equally to men and women. Modesty is an internal attitude that holds our bodies in high regard and recognizes them as either instruments of God or tools of sin (Romans 6:13). This conviction results in clothing and actions that conceal rather than reveal our physical comeliness. It cultivates an attitude of honor toward all parties involved, including our future spouse.

It is also a significant way we fight for our brother's purity, and we have the responsibility to fight well.

Whatever you see, in some manner, belongs to you. It doesn't cost you anything to repeat a line from a movie or replay in your head a particularly exciting scene. This is the way it is with our bodies. Those mental pictures of you belong to everyone who sees you. They can pull them up in their minds whenever they want. And men in particular (I am told) have a hard time keeping those images pure, especially when the clothes are too tight, too skimpy, or too sheer.

This is something women have to weigh every day. It's easy for us to see men's struggle and simply mock them as sexually driven animals. Or we realize the right clothes attract the attention and admiration we crave (or at least think we do). But regardless, when we, as women, ignore modesty in how we dress, we make it easy for men to justify their lustful desires and say, "The woman You gave me, God—it's her fault." Or each of us can individually choose to protect and encourage our brothers by our dress.

I was at a worship service recently, and I noticed the lead female vocalist was dressed between a Goth and a hipster. Then it hit me: she had purposefully dressed for modesty. She had dressed in layers, from her long and short sleeves to her layered skirts. I would probably not seriously consider wearing a single article of clothing she had on, but she had seemingly selected them aware that "modesty is a virtue that shows love to others and brings glory to God through appropriate dress."[5]

Modesty is not confined to a style or even an era of clothing. It is a reflection of a woman's heart that loves God, loves her brothers, and loves her husband.

But I have a confession: I find male modesty attractive. Men have much less opportunity to display modesty than women, and it's honestly rare for a man to realize someone shouldn't see part of his body. A man putting his shirt back on when we are both out running shows me respect. A fitness instructor wearing pants under his shorts speaks of his striving for excellence. I instinctively approve of purposeful modesty. And when God sees our modest dress and attitudes as women, He also approves.

Modesty coupled with the mind and attitude of Christ is always beautiful.

"Let nothing be done through selfish ambition or conceit, but in lowliness of mind let each esteem others better than himself. Let each of you look out not only for his own interests, but also for the interests of others" (Philippians 2:3–4).

Modesty coupled with the mind and attitude of Christ is always beautiful. From this mindset, modesty is a self-sacrificial gift of humility and love, a reflection of Jesus Christ.

——— REFLECT ———

What is your attitude toward the concepts of modesty? With Christ as your ultimate example, honestly evaluate: Does this attitude reflect Christ's love toward you to those around you?

PRAY

Ask God to open your eyes and teach you how to be modest in support of your Christian brothers and sisters as they seek to honor God with pure thoughts, attitudes, and actions.

TAKE A SINGLE STEP

Pick one area you know you need to be more supportive in (becoming a wiser sister or prayer warrior, servanthood, or modesty). Choose one way to do this, and start today.

Confession 24

A FAIRY-TALE ENDING

ONCE UPON A TIME IN a secret kingdom, which you could find if you knew the way, there was a princess. Her Father the King gave her beautiful dresses, wonderful food, and an impressive palace.

The only thing she didn't have was a prince. And that was what she wanted more than anything in the world. "All my friends have princes." She pouted.

"You are not your friends. And I am not their Father." The King often repeated this pointedly.

The princess tried different ways of asking. "Can I go look for a prince? I could attend the ball in the neighboring kingdom."

"And what do you think would happen if you looked for a prince?" The King smiled.

"I would find one."

"Exactly. And how would you know he was your prince?" The King's eyebrow cocked to the side.

The princess knew this answer. "My heart would tell me so. I already know I want him taller than Anne's prince and as handsome as Beth's and—"

The patient King sighed. "My daughter, if all you want is what someone else has, you will always be unhappy."

"But I am already unhappy, Daddy."

The King picked up a snow globe. "If you shake this snow globe and say someone's name, you will see what they think they want."

The delighted princess shook the snow globe, saying one of her friends' names. "Cathy!" A scene immediately appeared: the princess's palace, Anne's stunning yellow dress, and Beth's beautiful hair. But Cathy had a huge castle, a lovely voice, and a more practical dress.

The princess was confused. How could Cathy want what Anne and Beth had? The princess thought of other names.

"Diana . . . no . . . no, that's dumb. She just got married." The princess looked thoughtful. "But I have always thought I would like her . . ."

"Focus, daughter."

She nodded, then said Diana's name. And Cathy's mansion with all its books appeared inside the snow globe alongside Anne's husband. The princess was surprised. "Diana just got that beautiful house and a great husband!"

"It's not what you have that makes you happy but if you are happy with what you have," the King replied.

"Does that apply to princes?"

"Yes, and unicorns." The King smiled wisely.

I am happy being single most of the time. (I presume I am as happy as much of the time as any married person.) But I have found that something consistently makes me unhappy. Every time my mind indulges in envying friends who are married, this nurtures a restlessness and discontent. I grow angry with God and unhappy with myself whenever I compare myself to others.

And I, if I do say so myself, am a master comparer. I can compare my single life to your single life, your previous single life, and your married life. My comparisons don't even have to be based in reality. I can compare my imagined married life to your prospective married life, your current married life, or the married life I have imagined for you.

See, I told you—I am very good. Comparing our lives with theirs is a game most of us play every day, unless we are seriously on guard. We have practiced this game since we were old enough to realize her dress is prettier than mine or his bike is newer.

The problem is, you always lose this game. And it's no fun playing a game if you always lose.

James tells it like it is:

> Where do wars and fights come from among you? Do they not come from your desires for pleasure that war in your members? You lust and do not have. You murder and covet and cannot obtain. You fight and war. Yet you do not have because you do not ask. You ask and do not receive, because you ask amiss, that you may spend it on your pleasures. (James 4:1–3)

Point 1: Our comparisons are driven by lust—the desire to have.

This is not confined to sex. You can lust for houses or lands, love or validation, respect or approval. You can be driven by your desire to have more of anything—money, ministry, or mud pies. And discontent stems from these cravings.

Point 2: Lust is a mob boss.

Your debts are forever, and they're never letting you go—you always owe more. Even if you allow lust to devour you and make casualties of those you love, you cannot obtain what you seek because lust cannot be satisfied.

Point 3: Coveting (comparing) will not give you what you want, but it will wreak havoc with what you have.

It is a double-edged sword that simultaneously cuts down the comparer and the comparee. Observe: "Her stubby little fingers look so fat shoved into that wedding band. My fingers would never look like that."

In attempting to make myself feel better because I feel inferior, I have found that she is my superior because even with her pudgy fingers, she is married. And now, in my mind, we are both damaged goods—she because of how her ring looks, and me because of my lack of ring.

Point 4: Ask God. If you are fighting a battle with sexual desires, ask God.

If you are overwhelmed by loneliness, ask God. If you are struggling with doubt, ask God. Not so you can feel better and get on with your life but so you can be freed to live a Christ-centered life.

A woman named Paige once prayed, "Dear Lord, please help me be content being single, and make me . . ."

DING! DING! Her phone chirped as it blinked and did everything short of setting off flares.

"Ohhh, myperfectmatch.com thinks he and I would be a good fit! He's cute. Five feet, eleven inches . . . I like it. Flips burgers at the Bad Batch Burger . . . I can live with that. Likes to . . . aquarium spear fish . . . That's odd, but . . . okay. Click here to go on a date with . . . What's his name? Guy Discontent?"

Paige's prayer started out well, but her prayer had a problem: it wasn't a real prayer. She prayed for contentment, but then chucked trusting God out the window by continuing to act desperate and discontented with her status.

Prayer is a powerful privilege. It is access to the throne room of God, not another name for wishing or worrying or obsessing (i.e., pretend prayers). Wishing is evidence that I don't trust God's goodness. Worrying is proof that I don't really believe God's greatness. And obsessing is my assertion that I am really in control and can do better than God. True prayers change us.

How often have you prayed and asked God to give you contentment? Or wisdom, or guidance, or peace, or hope, or comfort? If you are like me, it is easy to ask, but then, because you feel the same, you go away and act exactly the same. That is a pretend prayer—a prayer that says "I trust God" but never really sets control in God's hands.

Paige said all the right words but didn't back them up with action.

If you are expecting to adopt a puppy (something I don't recommend because full-grown dogs are so much less work), you get ready to adopt a puppy. You buy food, dishes, a bed, a house, a collar, and a leash. You research training and puppy classes in your area. You find out where the nearest dog parks are. And you puppyproof your house and yard and warn the neighbors so everyone is prepared for when you bring your puppy home. When we pray, we should do the same: expect and prepare to receive an answer to that prayer.

If we, like Paige, ask God for contentment, we should cancel our membership with the local speed-dating pool, stop spending every waking minute on myperfectmatch.com, and trust that God will provide everything we need to minister for Him (2 Corinthians 9:8). If we aren't ready to do these things, we should be honest with ourselves and tell God the truth: "Dear God, please make me happy being single until I can fix my singleness. Amen."

I confess: I have prayed lots of pretend prayers. Sometimes because I am ignorant of the true state of my motives and desires (like the princess and Paige), but often because I pray flippantly. For example, I ask for wisdom but then walk away from praying indecisive and consumed by minutiae.

I act like my prayers are useless. But since God has already promised wisdom to those who ask Him (James 1:5), when we ask, we should study God's Word and seek godly counsel. Then we should move forward in confidence that God is keeping His word and providing the wisdom He promises.

It's the same with requesting guidance and peace or hope and comfort (2 Corinthians 1:3 and Hebrews 6:18). God has already promised these things (Isaiah 58:11 and John 14:27). So when we ask God for what He has clearly promised (like His presence—Hebrews 13:5), we need to trust and live like He keeps His promises, because He does!

And even when we pray for what we are not assured of (such as a life partner for ourselves or others), we can be sure God will answer in His time, for our good (Psalm 34:10), and according to His will (1 John 5:14–15). He is a faithful God (Deuteronomy 7:9). When God says yes, we can be confident it is for our good and the glory of His kingdom. And when God says no, we can be content, knowing His decision is for our good and the glory of His kingdom.

> The LORD has appeared of old to me, saying:
> "Yes, I have loved you with an everlasting love;
> Therefore with lovingkindness I have drawn you."
> (Jeremiah 31:3)

When we truly pray, we are relying on God to intervene. Here, at God's throne, we are changed. All of us can abandon any problem, leave any dream, and relinquish any worry at the feet of the King of all of creation. No excuse or justification for continuing to fret or fear. We can now live in joy and contentment at all times—because the almighty King is our Husband, and He loves us.

REFLECT

In His Word, God has given us many exceedingly great and precious promises (2 Peter 1:4). Pick one and think about how that promise can change how you pray. For example, take "those who seek the LORD shall not lack any good thing" from Psalm 34:10. When you pray for a good thing, it makes sense to also ask God to help you seek Him to know a good thing when you see it.

PRAY

Pray through the promise that you picked above. As you pray, consider what you should do in response to your prayer.

TAKE A SINGLE STEP

Each time you pray throughout the next week, ask yourself: If I just prayed a real prayer, what should I do?

For example: "Thank You, God, for this food, and bless it to our bodies so we can serve You. Amen." If this is a true prayer, you will try not to waste the food. (This doesn't necessarily mean you eat it all; you may save some for the next meal, freeze some, or give your dog a treat.) You will share your food if and when given the opportunity because you are grateful to God for it and recognize it is for His service. You will also eat a balanced diet and not overeat or undereat because you are asking God to help the food nourish your body and enable you to serve Him.

CONFESSIONS

OF THE

SOUL

My soul magnifies the Lord,
And my spirit has rejoiced in God my Savior.

LUKE 1:46–47

Confession 25

SURPRISED BY LOVE

Have you ever been impatiently waiting, and then something else comes along to distract you, making time seem to evaporate? Kids do this all the time. At first you can't make them happy doing something, and then they get into it and you can't pry them away.

Here is a confession (that hopefully you do not relate to): I'm childish. At numerous points in my life, God has had to drag me kicking and screaming from one stage to the next. My default position is to hold on to what I've got rather than let myself be surprised by my Redeemer's great love. This is a lesson Jane understands a whole lot better than I do.

Jane ambled over to the apple tree where a leg stuck out. She had been wanting to do just what the rancher was doing. Balanced on a large limb, he was funneling pretty red apples gently to the ground.

Jane eyed a shiny apple. "May I have that?"

"Sure. Plenty more up here." The voice was muffled by leaves.

"Thanks." Jane nosed the rest of the fruit into a pile.

A light shower of apples fell through the tree limbs. "Jackpot!" The cowboy's excitement attracted a few colts nearby.

Jane laughed as the younger horses came over and were soon rooting around the lower branches.

"Well, thanks for the help, gentlemen." The man slowly backed his boots out of the apple boughs. "That should be enough to share, don't you think?"

"Yes, sir." The paint colt tossed an apple to his friend. "I think we can find some hungry horses."

"Perfect." The man smiled as he slipped to the ground. "Thanks for your help, Jane."

"Oh, my pleasure." Jane finished her apple. "Have you had one yet?"

"Figured I'd get one eventually." The rancher's eyes twinkled. "So it seems we have something in common. We both love working the ranch."

Jane nodded. "It feels good to work hard for others."

"How about that—we've had a whole conversation and you haven't mentioned your horn once."

Jane skewered an apple and held it out to the rancher. "Maybe it's because I have learned to love other things."

Can you relate to Jane's feeling of contentment? If you are like me, you vacillate between impatience and contentment. Some days we are barely scraping by. On those days, God's love seems distant, and romantic love seems so far away, it may as well be impossible. But there are also days we wish we had more of. Days when Love is so close, we wonder why we ever desired a human lover.

And then, for some of us, there will be a day when Jane's story might look a bit more like this.

🐎

Jane ambled over to the apple tree. She had been wanting to do just what that chestnut horse was doing. Balanced on his hind feet, head up in tree limbs, he knocked an apple to the ground.

Jane eyed the shiny apple. "May I have that?"

"Sure. Plenty more up here." The voice was muffled by leaves.

"Thanks." Jane nosed the rest of the fruit into a pile as a small, red shower fell through the tree limbs.

"Jackpot!" the stallion trumpeted, attracting a few colts nearby.

Jane laughed as the younger horses came over and were soon rooting around the lower limbs.

"Well, thanks for the help, gentlemen." The chestnut slowly backed his hooves out of the apple boughs. "That should be enough to share, don't you think?"

"Yes, sir." The paint colt tossed an apple to his friend. "I think we can find some hungry horses."

"Perfect." The chestnut smiled as he slipped to the ground, still partially obscured by the apple tree. "I didn't catch your name," he said in Jane's direction.

"Oh, I'm Jane." Jane nudged an apple in his direction. "Have you had one yet?"

The bigger horse shrugged and smiled again. "Figured I'd get one eventually since the rancher sent me to pick them." His head seemed to catch on something briefly before he separated from the tree. "My name's Finley."

Jane felt her mouth drop open. Finley was a unicorn!

"Oh!" She blushed. "Finley's a nice name."

"It is, isn't it?" Finley laughed. "So, it seems we have something in common."

"Really?" Jane didn't meet his eyes.

He winked. "Yup. We both like apples."

How Jane's story ends I will leave up to you.

Especially since we all know there's a long way to go between two unicorns meeting and two unicorns marrying. And it's a process we unicorns should at least think about. We'd be surprised if our Rancher sends a unicorn our way, but we want to be savvy too.

How? Let me tell you a story to illustrate. But first, if I may brag for just a minute: I looked awesome. I had on a lime-green IRONMAN shirt—as in running, swimming, and biking—with a red hat advertising heavy construction equipment. My sling backpack matched the look I was going for, but what pulled everything together was the 9mm handgun that hung on my right hip with two extra magazines (which gun people call mags).

I was attending my first three-day handgun course. During those three days, I put four hundred rounds of ammo through that gun and stared down its short barrel for hours trying to do the same thing: hit the target, specifically the bull's-eye.

For a handgun, a bull's-eye is generally no more than a few square inches. To hit the bull's-eye, everything has to be right.

- Focus. If you are distracted, who knows where that bullet is going.
- Breathing. While shooting, breathing can cause your muzzle to rise and fall. So a marksman consciously times his breathing.
- Sight picture. Put the front sight even with and evenly between the back sights—no other configuration will work to hit that target.
- Target. If you are shooting your neighbor's circle, there is no way to hit your bull's-eye.
- Position. With a loaded weapon, you always face downrange. Nothing good happens facing any other direction.

- Grip. If you are gripping your handgun too tightly, it will rotate and throw your bullet to the side of your target. If your grip is too loose, the gun will jump back, and you will lose control. (This is called muzzle rise or muzzle flip.)
- Emotions. Even if it is fast, your trigger pull has to be steady and controlled. If you are anticipating the shot (i.e., scared of the boom), the muzzle is going to dip, and you will miss low.

The perfect shot is amazingly like a Christian's love life: it is a lot of work, but it's all worth it. And there is nothing better than hitting a bull's-eye.

Focus, Breathing, and Sight Picture

The Christian life (and love life) are always centered on Christ. Single, dating, courting, married, or widowed, we never shift our focus away from Him. Too often in love we try to hit a bull's-eye by taking our focus off Christ and putting it on our new relationship. This is like taking your eyes off the target. You'll never hit the center that way.

Making a shot requires steady breathing as well. Our breathing must be conscious and undistracted. A Christian spinster breathes by daily saturating herself in the Word of God and communing with God in prayer, service, and fellowship with other believers (particularly in church). Through some parts of life, these habits can become second nature. But during romantic relationships that distract, these habits must be purposefully pursued so Jesus Christ our Savior remains our steady and primary focus.

Many weapons are point and shoot, but if you'd like to hit what you are aiming for, lining up the sights is imperative. This is called a sight picture. A relationship that focuses on Jesus, paired with the desire for God's will and His glory in your life, is your sight picture. When all three are in alignment—Christ has preeminence, you are fulfilling God's known will, and you are honoring God in your life—you can take your shot *and* hit what you are aiming for.

Target and Position

Whatever you are shooting at is your target. "Target acquired" is the military way of saying, "I've got him in my crosshairs." However, target acquisition does not mean it is the correct target. Many singles are looking for any target. (We will ignore motives for the moment.) But in love, the Bible gives us clear instructions as to which targets are not fair game. A person of the same sex—she's not the one for you. A person already married—he's not for you. And a person who is not a Christian of growing maturity—he's not for you either.

And here is where facing downrange is critical. If Christians surround themselves with non-Christians, they are not even facing the correct direction to find their ideal target. They may end up shooting themselves or someone else but nothing good can happen. There is no way to hit a target with your weapon pointed the wrong way.

Grip

In physics, recoil is the equal and opposite force when a ballistic is fired. It can be almost nothing, or it can be enough to rip your arm off. Your grip braces against this force.

Blissfully unaware of recoil, some beginners do not grip their weapon firmly enough, which results in bruises, strains, and sprains. But most importantly they can lose control.

Singles, especially teenagers, who have never been in a relationship can be caught off guard by the intensity of the emotions awakened and the strength of those feelings. Just like a noncommittal grip on a gun, a love recoil can cause lasting damage and lead the gullible into devastating sin and its consequences. This is something we have, unfortunately, all witnessed in out-of-wedlock pregnancies, rushed weddings, broken hearts, and destroyed friendships.

Which is why it is tempting for most marksmen to have a death grip on their weapon. Because they want control . . . hello! The problem is that this kind of control pulls their gun off target—so they are in control but can't hit what they are aiming at. The proper grip on a handgun pushes away from your body and pulls back at the same time to stabilize your shot. In other words, it is self-controlled (seems vaguely familiar . . .).

Self-control in relationships is rarely mentioned in secular circles, and if it is, it is often ridiculed. It is hardly mentioned in Christian ones, and if it is, it is often overly simplified (i.e., don't have sex before marriage). Self-control is not simple. It is neither easy to accomplish nor confined to a single part of life.

Self-control is wise. But it is not fun, unless you count all the problems avoided. Self-control can't be completely spontaneous, because it takes intentional planning to vanquish temptation. Self-control is patient and is definitely not immediately gratified. And—hopefully, this will make you think—self-control is what enables us to be courageous, because self-control puts others and their needs ahead of what I need or want.

Spiritually, self-control is made possible by proper focus, breathing, and sight picture. Practically, it has a lot to do with motives, which are often expressed in questions of timing. Do I enter a relationship if I know one or both of us is not ready to be married? If the answer is yes, what am I really trying to get? And is that motive pure? (Hint: the answer is almost always no.)

So I am already in a relationship—how much time should we be spending together? Are other foundational relationships suffering? And if yes, has my focus and sight picture slipped? Have I made my significant other an idol, or has he done so to me?

A relationship is like a handgun: your grip must be balanced to hit the target and glorify God.

Emotions

You are almost there—you are keyed in, your breathing is in sync, your sight picture is perfect, you are facing downrange, you have acquired the (right) target, your grip is self-controlled, and you are at the ready. Ready to pull the trigger, steady and controlled—BANG! Bull's-eye.

When pulling the trigger of a gun, you want to be poised but relaxed so that you don't lose control when the gun goes off. You are trying to surprise yourself so there isn't time at the last second to move or jerk and thus cause the bullet to stray. That's the idea in Christian courtship: surprised by love. It is also a theme of the Song of Solomon. (Why else would it say multiple times to not awaken love until it pleases?)

I want to be surprised by love, and I already have been.

I may never enjoy the love of a man. But I am surprised on a daily basis by the love of my Savior. He speaks His love to me through His Word and His Spirit. His love notes are a beautiful flower breaking through the city sidewalk or a random act of kindness from a stranger. His constant presence brings peace and clarity to the hardest moments.

Christ's love for us knows no limits or boundaries, and if we fail to be enamored with this Love, who laid aside His glory, took up His cross, and gave up His life for us, we are truly missing the greatest love we could ever know. This is the love He desires to see reflected in our lives. As the king tells his daughter in the parable *The True Princess*, "It is love that marks the true daughter of the king."[1]

And that is our goal as we prepare for romance. We obey all God's instructions. We hone a dedicated focus on Christ. We walk with Him in joy and honor. We live for the glory of God and the service of

His kingdom and surround ourselves with other Christians seeking Christ.

And *bang*—you realize together, you and he would be a power-house, and you decide to accept his offer to begin a relationship. It's a real-life Jane and Finley.

Yes, emotions and endorphins will run high. But this whole time you've been practicing self-control, and self-control is wise, so you know not to trust your own strength. Instead, you corral your emotions with checks and balances: spending little time alone as a couple (or you may realize no time alone is best), maintaining thriving relationships with God and others, and deepening your relationship in other ways.

You've taken the shot. Now is the moment of truth—time to check the target. Call a cease-fire on the firing line, walk down, and evaluate. Did you hit the bull's-eye?

Remember, there's nothing sweeter than a perfect shot.

> Let him kiss me with the kisses of his mouth—
> For your love is better than wine. (Song of Solomon 1:2)

REFLECT

How do you see and experience God's love on a daily basis?

PRAY

Place all your romantic relationships at the target of God's feet and leave them there.

TAKE A SINGLE STEP

Evaluate your life point by point with God.

Focus: Is it on Christ?

Breathing: Are you daily seeking God's face in His Word and prayer?

Sight picture: Is your goal God's will and His glory?

Target: Is the man you are considering romantically approved by God? If you aren't in such a relationship, Jesus is your target. Are you serving and living in fellowship with Christ?

Position: Who are you surrounding yourself with?

Grip: Are you setting wise boundaries and cultivating self-control to maintain focus on Jesus?

Emotions: When was the last time you were surprised by God's love? Are you ready to receive His love today?

Confession 26

CHRISTMAS EVE AND SINGLE

IF YOU WATCH HALLMARK MOVIES, then you know "Christmas Eve and single" is the goal of no Hallmark movie . . . ever. And I have a couple of confessions.

First, I watch Hallmark movies, especially between November and January—at least until I get sick of puppy love disconnected from a relationship with Jesus and reality. Second, perhaps you never have, but I admit: I have prayed several Hallmark Christmas prayers at various times of the year.

A Hallmark Christmas prayer sounds something like this: "Dear Lord, I really want a husband for Christmas . . . or by December 31 at the latest. Don't disappointment me—please." As desperate as that looks on paper, it sounds even more pitiful in person. A Hallmark Christmas prayer leaves the pray-er focused fully on herself and hungry for what is coming in the future instead of being focused on God and others, and grateful for all the gifts God has given her right now.

And that is a sorry mindset going into the season of celebrating God's greatest gift to mankind. That first Christmas night no one knew how wonderful this gift truly was. Even later, when the magi showed up with their extravagant presents, it was just beginning to become obvious: history would rise and fall on this child.

The wise men traveled through hundreds of miles of desert on little more than a sophisticated hunch that the King of the Jews had been born. And as good as their education and research were, the professors of the world needed the Word of God because deduction cannot tell you God's plans.

The religious leaders in Jerusalem knew God's promises so well they immediately supplied the answer to the question posed by the scholars. But those same priests were unwilling to travel even the six miles from Jerusalem to Bethlehem to see if God's Messiah had truly come.

The wise men traveled half the world with priceless treasures that "just so happened" to declare Christ's identity. The frankincense displayed the deity and priesthood of Jesus. The sovereignty and kinghood of the Messiah was declared by the gold. And the sacrifice of the suffering Savior was symbolized in the myrrh.

But the religious leaders who were supposed to be expecting Him brought the Messiah nothing, and even given thirty more years, most of them never made it to worship at His feet.

But when the magi made it to Jesus, they responded the only way possible. They rejoiced. God had counted them worthy to receive the gift of His Son and to give their best gifts back to Him. And they fell on their knees in worship. There is no other place you can find yourself when you realize that by the grace of God, you are just where you are supposed to be: in the center of His plans.

The wise men were well respected, well educated, and well-to-do. Using these blessings, they sought out and accepted God's invitation to His Son's birth. Hidden among their entourage, the kings brought costly gifts and international publicity for the newborn King of Kings. But the wise men were not God's only guests.

The Lord announced Christ's birth to a gaggle of shepherds. The shepherds were almost social outcasts, known by few and ignored by most. Lacking money, resources, and education, these men had little to recommend them for God's guest list. What could they possibly bring? Like many, I relate less to the magi and rather acutely to the shepherds (especially while watching sappy movies). What extravagant thing could I bring God that would make people sit up and take notice? I have no children. No home. No husband. No couple's ministry or shared mission. Nothing.

And that question isn't restricted to the most wonderful time of the year. I was reading Paul's letters one autumn only to be challenged with that same question. What is the biggest proof I trust God and my faith is real? What is my best evidence that God is good, gracious, and worthy of worship? Or put differently, what is my greatest gift to God?

Of course, no gift we give is apart from Him. "For all things come from You, and of Your own we have given You" (1 Chronicles 29:14). The only gifts we can give are a result of His blessings of strength, creativity, and opportunity. But still, I couldn't help but fixate on this dilemma. It seemed like I didn't have anything to bring God.

I knew God said being single was a gift equal with marriage (or even better—1 Corinthians 7). But for the longest time, I simply couldn't accept that because I didn't feel it was true. Instead, what I felt was conflicted, as if with every biblical passage or sermon on marriage and family God was asking me to give Him something I didn't have. High expectations are fine, but if there is one thing I dislike in life, it's expectations that are impossible to meet.

When I was in high school, I did competitive speech and debate. I loved getting back a good ballot—the form judges filled out. A good ballot would tell you a few things you did well and one or two specific things to improve upon. But the worst thing was getting back a ballot that said something like, "The team next door was so loud, I couldn't hear you." Or worse, "I like male speakers better."

Feedback that hinged on something I couldn't change was frustrating. The circumstances of the debate round were completely outside of my control. I couldn't change them any more than I could change my sex or my height. And this is what I felt each time I sat in the pews and heard or read Paul's instructions to families, like God wanted everyone to be married with kids.

But in reality, if God asks us for something, He will enable us to give it. Doubtless His commands require endurance, submission, and sacrifice, but He only ever asks us for what we can give. And He knows precisely what we can give Him, because He's the One who gave it to us in the first place. He isn't in heaven hoping we get married faster so we can respect our husbands or love our children.

On the contrary, if He withholds an opportunity, He expects something else from us. And to continue pursuing "it" (marriage, children, or so on) to glorify God would be self-defeating and self-aggrandizing.

It is self-defeating because our goal is to please God, so we should seek to fulfill His desires for us. Otherwise it is like giving someone a gift because you want to use it. It may be good for some laughs (or a blow-up argument), but it rarely works out well in a human sense, and it doesn't work out well with God either. To make it worse, an attitude that says God would be better served if we got married or had a family is a subtle form of self-worship. We have now elected ourselves to the position of deciding what God wants from us, regardless of what He has said and demonstrated to the contrary.

My reaction to this realization was less than flattering. "Fine then." I pouted and shut my Bible. "But if my greatest gift is not what I want it to be, namely marriage and a family, what is it? How do I demonstrate with my life that God is good and His ways are good?"

"What do you have?" God's Spirit asked me what Elisha asked the widow in 2 Kings 4:1–7.

"Nothing!" was the widow's reply. "I have sold everything except a jar of oil." Hers was a desperate situation, but Elisha didn't go visit the local magistrate or take up an offering. No. He simply told her to gather as many containers as she could, fill them with oil she already had, and sell it.

That was plum crazy. There was not enough oil to do diddly. But the widow obeyed anyway. Maybe she figured the plan would either fail or God would do a miracle. (Really, what other options were there?)

And of course, we know the story. God took what she had and filled every single pot, bottle, and bowl with oil for her and her sons, who were now eyewitnesses: God was totally enough.

"What do you have?"

I felt as if the Holy Spirit was grilling me. "Nothing! No house, no husband, no children!" I rehearsed in my mind: *I can't give God a godly marriage. I can't present to Him my faithfully discipled children. I can't bring Him a couples or families ministry or a life as a pastor's wife.*

"All I have is that I'm single." Empty resignation filled my words and my being.

His Spirit caught me in a moment when I was too tired to fight anymore. "Yes. So . . ."

I paused. My brain hurt trying to synthesize all God's truths, and finally I just made my best guess. "My singleness is my greatest gift?" As soon as I said it, I knew it was right—a light had come on and given me a snapshot of God's perspective. It was the Lord who had gifted to me the opportunity of my aloneness. So my greatest gift back to Him must also be my singleness as reflected in my worship, words, and work.

In Worship

Worship is not merely the songs we sing or the words we say on Sundays. Worship is a condition of the heart. A worship-full heart overflows with praise to God for His love, His faithfulness, and His presence. It protects us from becoming self-reliant, because habitual worship exalts in the Lord, His power, His justice, and His wisdom.

The call to worship is certainly not confined to singles. But our praise looks different based on the experiences God has sustained us through. I cannot worship God for His blessings of husband or children (at least not yet). But I can and will bear witness that, for more than thirty years, it's just been me and Him, and He has always been faithful. A patient teacher, loving Father, and mighty refuge is my God.

And that is the worship of my heart.

> I will extol You, my God, O King;
> And I will bless Your name forever and ever.
> Every day I will bless You,
> And I will praise Your name forever and ever.
> Great is the LORD, and greatly to be praised;
> And His greatness is unsearchable. (Psalm 145:1–3)

In Words

Mark 5:1–20 tells the story of a Gentile man who was hopelessly demon-possessed. Men couldn't control him, let alone save him. He lived alone among the tombs, a dead man walking.

The previous night there had been a bad storm; that probably made the possessed man even more miserable than normal. But that storm also blew a certain boat to his part of Galilee, a boat carrying a Jewish man named Jesus. The one person in the world who could give this man life appeared on his . . . tombstep.

What was impossible for men wasn't even a challenge for Jesus. The demons were sent packing, the man was set free, and Jesus gave the man a mission: "Go home to your friends, and tell them what great things the Lord has done for you, and how He has had compassion on you" (Mark 5:19).

Have not you and I been set free? Do we not have the same commission to tell others the good news about what God has done for us and can do for them?

Yes! We do.

I may be alone in this world, but I testify to this: no good thing has God ever withheld from me (Psalm 84:11). He has given His Son to die in my place so my sins may be forgiven and I may walk with God now and forever in heaven. (This is also true for you if you are trusting in Christ to rescue you from your sins and give you peace with God.)

He has gifted me with faith to believe in Jesus and given me a book of His promises and instructions. Even though I've been impatiently waiting for His timing, the more I wait, the more assured I become that God has kept and is keeping all of His promises to me and will keep them for you.

Who should I tell that God is enough? Anyone who will listen. Whether that is praying for coworkers, encouraging friends, loving the least of these, or serving others at church, it is our privilege to sing the praises of our God to a world that is dying to meet Him.

In Work

People always clapped enthusiastically for the "good" testimonies at church. You know, the ones where Jesus saved someone from gross immorality or the lifestyle of a serial arsonist. And I was definitely one of those kids who listened and thought, *If only I could have been a heroin addict! Or an illegal arms dealer!* Maybe you were one of those kids too.

It's interesting how we think, even as adults, that God must be more pleased with dramatic stories . . . or dramatic service. Is God desirous that the international politician come to believe in Christ as Lord and Savior? Yes, but no more so than the kid down the street.

Is God pleased when a single woman goes to the deepest, darkest part of the Amazon rain forest? Yes, but no more so than you or I joyfully doing what He has called us to do at our workplaces, at our churches, and in our communities. And that calling may not lead us to exotic places, but God is calling each of us to service right now, in the right way, and with the right motives.

Right now. Each of us is tripping over multiple opportunities to serve: at church, at work, with friends and family, and in the ministries we support. We just need to start giving of ourselves. Maybe it's our hands to clean or bake. It may be our feet to do yard work or ears to listen. Perhaps it's our mouth to teach or encourage, or our eyes to see someone who needs a friend.

In the right way. My pastor preached on this one Sunday: "Do all things without complaining and disputing" (Philippians 2:14). Or in other words, serve with the attitude of Jesus (which is the first part of Philippians 2).

With the right motives. Service may gain us many things, including purpose and satisfaction, friends and a reprieve from our loneliness, and even earthly and heavenly rewards. But our motive is to please Christ. We serve others because Christ served us. Serving God is not a great way to meet single men (believe me, I've tried), solidify your retirement, or gain social media followers. But it is joy filled, satisfying, and tangible proof that we love and follow Jesus.

Through worship, words, and work, our singleness is transformed from a gift into a blessing to God, to ourselves, and to others. Someday soon it will be our greatest pleasure to lay this blessing down before God's heavenly throne—our absolute best made absolutely acceptable by Christ. In that moment, not a single sacrifice of our singleness will we regret.

REFLECT

What will it be worth in heaven to be able to say, "Lord, I know it is inadequate, but I have given You my greatest gift"?

PRAY

What is the worship of your heart? What words do you want to tell others about your amazing Savior? And what works are you pursuing for the glory of God? Express those to God.

TAKE A SINGLE STEP

Pick one way to worship God, speak of God, and work for God today, and do it! Bonus points if you hit all three at the same time.

Confession 27

PROVERBS 31 SERMONS

How many sermons have you heard on Proverbs 31? Most Mother's Day messages at least reference it, unless you are at my church on Mother's Day, then you may hear a message on Rahab, the harlot. Oh, the irony.

But the answer to that question is probably *quite a few*. What are single women supposed to do with those sermons? Do they even apply to us at all?

For years this is how I applied them:

Alisha's To-Do List

1. Become virtuous.
2. Card wool, spin flax (after I learn what it is), and weave.
3. Learn to cook, bake, and import exotic foods.
4. Be a morning person.
5. Study investment banking while growing a garden.
6. Compete in triathlons.
7. Make do with little to no sleep.
8. Find a distaff and spindle. (Note to self: check online.)

9. Help others.
10. Design and sew clothing.
11. Dress like a fashion designer.
12. Operate a small business and figure out embroidery.
13. Be wise and kind.
14. See the eye doctor—so I can watch over my household better.

This final checkbox was invisible. But it definitely existed:

15. Earn a great husband.

And before you think *That's ridiculous—no one would think that*, consider all the sermons you've heard on womanhood. Imagine sitting in the pew—with neither spouse nor little ones—taking detailed notes.

- Support and be submissive to your husband. *I can do that . . . maybe . . . I think.*
- Be modest. *Nailed this one!*
- Develop a gentle and quiet spirit. *I'm working on it . . .*
- Trust God. *Oh, Lord, help me trust You even more.*
- Obey. *If You say to get married—sure!*
- Love and train your children. *This is exactly what I want to do.*

Then the sermon ends, and you feel prepared to get married and have a dozen kids. You are ready. Every sermon on these topics confirms this to you.

You are willing to follow God's instructions to a T. You've done it right every time—in your imagination. You believe you have completed the preflight checklist and (cue the game-show-host voice) earned a godly husband!

But what if the sermon ends and you are left holding a list of requirements and feeling subpar and deflated? *Since I am not married, I can't be a Proverbs 31 woman. Does what I do even matter?* In this frame of mind, messages on marriage and family and children simply become painful ordeals to endure, after which you go home and lick your wounds.

Interestingly, both the emboldened and the depressed women above have viewed these passages in Scripture in the same single-dimensional (no pun intended) way. They are looking at them as pre-marriage to-do lists. And it's easy to see why. Those notes above look like lists of dos and don'ts to be successful and earn the right to a godly man, some wonderful children, and a fulfilling family life.

Clearly, these rabid note-taking singles have missed the point and the boat and the target and . . . You get the message.

Proverbs 31 is not a checklist. It is an inspirational description of God's design for a godly woman. Neither 1 Peter 3 nor Titus 2 are checklists (or fail-safe strategies to get married). They are instructions for those, both male and female, who are already married.

Singles are wise to pursue these godly character qualities, to prepare for the future and study God's direction for a joyful family and marriage. But to think you can fulfill "the requirements" in exchange for a godly spouse is like expecting your stellar math skills to get you the lead in a Broadway musical—they aren't connected to each other.

Every partner is human and will make mistakes. If the thought process is "I earned you through my excellent character and superior life skills" (which translates into "I am a worthy spouse"), what happens if the new husband is deemed unworthy?

Maybe the outcome is divorce, because I earned the right to a companion of similar, though-not-quite-as-good-as-me, caliber, so I will go find one. Or maybe the result is bitterness against God (and likely your spouse) because He (and he) owes me and didn't keep up His (or his) end of the bargain. Or maybe the outcome is an entitled marriage filled with condescension and a superiority complex—after all, I am the one who did all the right things.

Pick your poison, but it doesn't end well. If the underlying philosophy is wrong, the tactics will be poorly conceived, and the long-term battle plan will fail. But when the underlying philosophy is correct, strategies will be rooted in truth, and an accurate vision for the future is possible with God.

God's philosophy is that, whether future possibility or present reality, a godly spouse is from Him (Proverbs 19:14). They are not earned or found or made (for those of us who like to "fix" people). They are God's gift to be loved, respected (or valued), and enjoyed as a reflection of our gratitude to God for His good, perfect, and timely gift.

This is one way the Proverbs 31 woman does her husband good all the days of her life. As a wise single, she looked ahead and started viewing her husband correctly before he was even in the conversation. She knew he was a sinner saved by grace. She accepted him as God's gift given to her to respect (not remodel).

She realized "the most loving thing a wife can do for her husband is to pray for him," as author Melanie Chitwood says in her book *What a Husband Needs from His Wife*.[1] So why not start now? And even in her prayers, the Proverbs 31 woman understood a husband can never be earned.

That realization doesn't always take away the painful stab when listening to a Proverbs 31 sermon. But it does make it easier to give God a humble heart, which He loves, and the sacrifice of praise, of which He is always worthy.

REFLECT

How do the things on your daily to-do list demonstrate God's design for you?

PRAY

Submit yourself to God's working in your life, and ask for His help to fulfill His design for you. Request His protection against arrogance and selfishness when you succeed, and entreat His encouragement when you fail.

TAKE A SINGLE STEP

Read Proverbs 31 not as a checklist but as a description of a godly woman. What character qualities does she demonstrate? How does your life show those same qualities? (That's God working in your life!)

Confession 28

LESS GODLY = MORE MARRIED?

THE ED (EMERGENCY DEPARTMENT) WAS blowing up: patients were stacked to the ceiling, multiple ambulances were rolling in, and I was being pulled in six different directions when . . .

"Hey! When are you coming on a ride-along?" an EMT asked me as I nearly ran past.

"What?" I see lots of EMTs on a regular basis. I know most of them by face, and they know me. But I had never been invited on a ride-along, and I'd never seen this medic before.

"Come down to the station. You should hang out with us sometime." He was making his gurney with clean sheets. "You're always welcome."

"Uh, thank you." I racked my brain. *Do I know this guy from somewhere? He clearly thinks he knows me.*

"Hey, you want to get coffee sometime?"

"What?" I must have seemed pretty dim-witted. But maybe that was it: we didn't know each other. He was just angling for a date. "Oh, thanks, but I'll pass."

And I got out of there as quickly as possible. The conversation was so odd, the whole afternoon I kept coming back to it. It sure seemed like he knew me. But he didn't. Who else? *Bang!* It hit me. My newest coworker.

She had similar hair (though not as red as mine), was roughly my size, and, most importantly, visited a lot of the EMS posts in the area. They had probably only recently met, and with the novel coronavirus circling the globe, we were all masked and in the same scrubs. *An easy mistake to make*, I thought.

The next minute a wave of near panic washed over me. If this guy thought I was her, I just turned down a date for her. And worse—I shuddered—she would go on her usual rounds to provide EMS instruction and have no earthly idea why she was getting dirty looks from the men at this station who knew "she" had turned down a ride-along and date in the same conversation.

"Oh no!" I said out loud. Fortunately, she was working my next shift, and we had a conversation that started with "you know, I think I refused a date for you."

Thus are the pitfalls of being single in the workplace. I wonder if Jesus had those kinds of issues, because . . . ready for the trump card? Jesus was single and our perfect example of singleness. Untethered to a home, He willingly slept on the ground (Matthew 8:20) and traveled from town to town preaching, teaching, and healing people (Luke 9:6). He used His flexible schedule to devote time to prayer (Luke 5:16). Whatever God prompted Him to do, He did fully and willingly (Philippians 2:7–8).

Anyone who has read the Bible will notice a few things if they are paying attention. Ninety-nine percent (random, high percentage chosen for illustrative purposes only) of Bible characters are married. Of the 1 percent who aren't, about half are women. But male or female, most singles in the Bible are godly.

This is the point at which people are arguing either that "obviously" singles are super-Christians or that this is mere selection bias. Selection bias says singles in the Bible were selected to be in the Bible precisely because they were that godly, since there is no other reason to talk about an unmarried person.

As to the super-Christian argument, all Christians are called to be perfect (Matthew 5:48)—being married or single is not license to be anything else. Peter was married and a pillar of the Jewish Christian church, while Paul's world-changing ministry to the Gentiles was, in part, possible because he had no wife and children.

Even if it meant hunger, shipwreck, beatings, or danger, Paul was free to follow the Holy Spirit unencumbered. When he was thrown in jail and was unable to work, there was no one at home to suffer hunger. When he was driven out of a city, he could be lowered over a wall (Acts 9:25) without worrying about how his wife would find him. Paul could give his all to Christ because he had no competing responsibilities.

So maybe it is selection bias. But if it is, singles like you and me are walking in high and noble company. And we can find great encouragement in this godly cohort of unmarried servants of God. If you make a list of the godliest women in the Bible, particularly in the New Testament, approximately 50 percent were unmarried. (This does not hold true for men, however, as most of the godliest men were married: Abraham, Moses, David, Peter, and so on.)

Alisha's List of the Godliest Women in the Bible

> Miriam—presumed single
> Deborah—married (though there is some debate here)
> Hannah—married
> Abigail—married
> Anna—single (widowed)
> Mary the mother of Jesus—married
> Elizabeth—married
> Mary and Martha—both presumed single

Dorcas—presumed single
Lydia—presumed single
Priscilla—married
Phillip's four virgin daughters who prophesied—single

So based on this list, mathematically, godly women are at high risk of being perpetually single. And this observation brings up a sensitive discussion. (One that I had incorrectly assumed would be relevant to men until a reliable source assured me that, in his experience, men do not think this way.) If godly women appear more likely to be alone for the rest of their lives, and biblically this may be the case, and we really want to get married, can't we just be less godly?

Girls do this all the time in other parts of life. Not pretty enough—more makeup. Too tall—slouch. Not tall enough—heels. Too smart—act dumb. Too dumb—wear glasses. If being godly is a speed bump toward getting married, like being extraordinarily tall or inordinately smart, I'll just change my spiritual IQ and trim off a few godly habits.

The problem is that if you slouch long enough, you develop a stoop. Godliness, the character of God, is an outflow of the Holy Spirit in our lives. This is why in Galatians 5:22–23 it is the "fruit," not the "fruits," of the Spirit—that one fruit is godliness. If we purposefully hamper the Spirit's work in our lives and resist His grace to grow spiritually, it will damage our relationship with Christ and our spiritual IQ will be permanently stunted.

We see examples of this truth in our everyday lives. I once had a teenage patient whose father only spoke Spanish. But when we started talking with her in Spanish, she abruptly said in perfect English, "I don't speak Spanish." I still don't believe that she couldn't speak Spanish; I believe she wouldn't speak Spanish. And if you refuse to use a language (just like other skills), there will come a time when you are indeed unable to understand it.

If we refuse to listen and obey God's Spirit, there will come a time when we will be unable to understand Him. And if our approach to snagging a man is to ignore God, men have become our first priority. We are demonstrating our belief, deep inside, that a man will give us the future we want and fix our loneliness.

But in reality, it is only God who provides us a future and a hope (Jeremiah 29:11). It is God who never leaves us nor forsakes us (Hebrews 13:5). Anything else is an idol robbing God's place. And this is something God is never okay with, and we shouldn't be either, because we can't have fulfilling relationships with idols. But this approach of being less holy to be more hooked up is also ironic.

> ## So if we want to be gorgeous (and who doesn't?), press on to greater godliness, not faster marriage.

When we think to ourselves, *Well, I'll just be less spiritual so I will be more attractive to guys*, we are shooting ourselves in the foot. Not only are godly men (whom we would ideally like to marry) supposed to be seeking godly women, but the Bible tells us beauty is a defining trait of God's presence, because holiness is beautiful (1 Chronicles 16:29).

So if we want to be gorgeous (and who doesn't?), press on to greater godliness, not faster marriage. Everyone else may be doing whatever they can to get whatever they want, but you, O woman of God (married or unmarried), flee lust and greed, and pursue righteousness, godliness, faith, love, patience, and gentleness alongside those who also call upon God with pure hearts (1 Timothy 6:9–11; 2 Timothy 2:22).

That is God's road map for pursuing godliness, and godliness is profitable for all things (1 Timothy 4:8).

Businesses want to hire women of integrity, because they are responsible. People choose friends who are loving and gentle, because they are encouraging.

The church needs women intent on being faithful and pure, because these kinds of women build up the kingdom. So believe me, or better yet, believe God: godliness looks good on you.

REFLECT

Everyone has different struggles, and that's okay. Maybe you never even considered being less godly to get a man. But what compromises have you made or been tempted to make to get to marriage faster? Whatever your answer, invite God in to forgive you, guide you, and pull you back into His ideal.

PRAY

Take five uninterrupted minutes to meditate on the character of God and enjoy the beauty of His presence in prayer.

TAKE A SINGLE STEP

Jesus is our perfect example of singleness. Write down at least three things He did as a Christian single that you could do as well.

Confession 29

SINGLE PURPOSE

IF YOU ARE LIKE ME, you've sat looking at your bedroom, your apartment, your hotel room and wondered, *This can't be all God has for me, can it?*

I couldn't have been more than twelve when I decided I had to have a hope chest. It would fulfill my life and solidify my future. But without it, my life would be empty and pointless. Thus, my first hope chest was supplied: my dad's old navy locker. I painted it white and stenciled flowers on the top.

But by the time I was in my midteens, I realized that trunk was not only heavy enough to stop a bullet, but it was old and ugly. So I disposed of the chest and settled for something more practical. It was now my waiting-for-life-to-start plastic tub.

Romantic, I know. But that is the way our culture thinks. Life doesn't start until that special someone shows up. The old-timey way of saying this is that she is biding time until marriage.

For many of us, marriage has been idealized as the pinnacle of God's calling for His daughters. If someone isn't married, she is waiting—just waiting. No one really taught us that our status is a gift or how to use that gift to impact eternity, and everyone was more than willing to help us down the aisle. We didn't get much encouragement or kind words outside of the classic comment, "Don't worry. God will bring the right one." And at the end of the day, we were all left waiting—just waiting.

Hopefully you didn't, but I agreed with this way of thinking for more years than I want to confess. But the truth is this idea is a destructive, self-centered excuse and a bald-faced (and a bold-faced) distraction.

God has prescribed for us an unknown but finite number of days (Psalm 139:16). As a gift from God, each day is purposeful. We have a mission from God right now. It's a lie to believe unattached is merely a bridge to romance, love, and marriage.

God's design for singlehood is not like waiting in line at the DMV.

The line at the DMV has been the site of some of the most unproductive hours in my life so far. God's design for singlehood is not like waiting in line at the DMV. It is more like savoring one course of a gourmet meal: it isn't coming around again. God has specific plans for us today and every day that follows. He has goals for growth, for ministry, and for relationships, and they are always for our good.

God has designed this time to be enjoyed—like marveling at the view of Yosemite's Half Dome before summiting. The whole trip is meant to be meaningful, not just the time spent at the top (which is comparatively brief). Singleness is not a means to an end—marriage. It is a means to know and serve God. In the classic *The Practice of the Presence of God*, Brother Lawrence encourages us, "Abandon any other concerns, including any special devotion [like pursuing marriage] you've undertaken simply as a means to an end. God is our 'end.'"[1]

Singles need to uproot all lies that have infiltrated our thinking, especially those telling us our singleness is a deficit or a problem or a hurdle to jump before we can "live." It isn't. Singleness doesn't, by definition, isolate us. It doesn't make us unfit for service, as I have believed at various times. And it doesn't keep us from doing great things for God. God has included us, by name and by life circumstance, in His church. He sees our singleness as part of our qualifications for service and wants to use us to do great things, things others cannot do.

This is why biding time is a self-centered perspective of our lives. Our unmarried time isn't just for us. This time is for others. When Paul spoke to the Corinthians about marriage, he said the unmarried care for the things of God because this is what singles are supposed to do! We are not to be consumed with seeking a spouse. We are not to get sidetracked with all the things we could be doing because we are single: cars, shopping, golf, or sports. We are not to be neutralized by daydreaming, fantasizing, or throwing our own pity party.

We are the single-minded in pursuit of Christ. As such, we are called to build up Christ's church. So we have to be involved in that church. We are the unencumbered. We are supposed to be pushing Christ's kingdom forward. So we have to be investing ourselves and our assets in that kingdom. We are the advance guard; we need to engage in battle. Most of the church is distracted by many things. It cannot afford for us to be made irrelevant by lies or excuses that water down the crucial nature of our calling as God's singles. The church needs us to accept our clearly assigned mission, which is not to become married Christians.

"I don't feel like I fit in."

"The church doesn't want me."

"There isn't anything I can do that someone else can't."

"I don't have any experience."

We've all felt these things.

But the truth is, our mission is to walk worthy of Christ, fulfilling the good works God has prepared for us right now. "For we are His workmanship, created in Christ Jesus for good works, which God prepared beforehand that we should walk in them" (Ephesians 2:10).

When we make up excuses to explain why we can't do what God has told us to do, we justify our disobedience to our own detriment. And when we allow distractions (like the pursuit of marriage, entertainment, money, or other interruptions) to entice us away from our true purpose as God's singles, we rob God, His church, and ourselves of the blessings God desires to give. But when we wholeheartedly accept our calling, we glorify God, build up His body, and experience the abundant life He promises us.

Near the close of her book on marriage, *What a Husband Needs from His Wife*, Melanie Chitwood quips, "Our greatest joy is to be used by God, but that is sometimes also our greatest challenge."[2] Once we seize God's purpose in our lives, we have to learn to steward our time, effort, and resources to achieve His purposes. Here Christians face a double-edged risk. The first is much more common. It is the temptation to use what we have selfishly on entertainment, expensive doodads, and so on. The second is to say yes to everything and burn ourselves out and use up our resources. Both examples are not just poor stewardship; they are diametrically opposed to what Christ has designed for us.

A while back my family and I were at a family camp in southern Colorado. Having several hours before the evening session began, we went exploring and found a tiny lake with canoes.

So even though it was October, we threw on life vests, grabbed paddles, and jumped in canoes. About five minutes into our adventure, I grew tired of our side of the pond and decided to glide under the footbridge to the other side.

This was an excellent plan except one thing. My mom was in the front of the canoe.

"Just lay back!" I directed from behind her.

"There's not enough space!" she yelped from the front.

"Lay—" The rest of my words were obscured because instead of trying to lie back, my mom opted to dodge the bridge's struts.

Canoe, remember? *Splash.*

We flipped, and it was a cold walk back to the dorm, but an excellent time to consider some basic life lessons about balance:

1. Balance is important.
2. There are lots of things that can throw off our balance.
3. Canoeing brings this to a whole new level physically.
4. Stewardship brings this to a whole new level spiritually.

It takes balance to use your finances, possessions, relationships, and time wisely rather than from a place of self-centeredness. There are many attitudes toward stuff that will throw off this balance:

1. What I have belongs to me.
2. What belongs to me is best used to get more stuff.
3. Getting more stuff is the ultimate goal.

These are all hallmarks of self-centered stewardship. Life in America, even among Christians, whether single or married, demonstrates this approach in spades. It is the no-holds-barred, just-get-me-what-I-want approach to life. Alcohol. Drugs. Entertainment. All-consuming hobbies. Big hair and houses. Fancy cars and clothes. Our lives evidence this philosophy by our gratuitous self-indulgence and failure to produce the fruit of wisdom (James 3:13–18).

We refuse to tithe to the Lord "our" money—if there's any left over, maybe . . . Our lives are dedicated to producing great careers at the expense of vibrant faith. Our marriages are all about my satisfaction and happiness. We spend our time like it belongs to us, as though we could take a single breath on our own without divine enablement.

Christian singles who are not intentionally grounded in the Bible easily fall into selfish stewardship.

Perk up your ears the next time you hear someone say, "Well, if I do that for God [such as move, give money, do ministry], I couldn't do what I want." That is selfish stewardship speaking. Notice "I" is the subject and "God" is the object. It should be the opposite: "God" is the subject, and "I" am the object He is working on and using.

If self were a symbol, it would look like this: ●. A black hole. It is where the small-minded wallow and squander their vanishing days. (Too dramatic? Okay, I'll work on it.)

Black holes suck everything into them. Nothing escapes, and still its desire is infinite. It can never be satisfied—just like the lust or greed in the human heart (Proverbs 27:20).

But why did God, knowing all things, design our hearts with insatiable appetites? Answer: He placed within us this infinite desire for Himself—an infinite God (Ecclesiastes 3:11). Self-centered stewardship is a reflection of this insatiable core desire to *have*—a desire that can only be met in Jesus Christ.

Once Christ is truly our Lord, we are able to be wise stewards who

1. understand that it is all God's (1 Chronicles 29:16; Psalm 24:1);
2. use everything generously and prudently (Isaiah 32:8; Luke 19:11–27); and
3. focus on eternal treasures as the true goal (Matthew 6:19–20).

So how can we tell if we are being wise stewards?

Generosity is easy.

We pray, trust God, and then cheerfully give what we have purposed in our heart to give (2 Corinthians 9:7). And when we think we are withholding more than is right (Proverbs 11:24), we trust God and ask Him to make us generous, and then we give generously and joyfully.

Prudence is more difficult.

My parents started savings accounts for my siblings and me before we could understand the concept. Our little minds did not comprehend why it was better to invest the money in the big bank instead of just putting it in our piggy banks. If it's in the big bank, my money might exist somewhere, but I can touch, use, and taste the money in my piggy bank (pennies taste awesome!); isn't that better? My parents didn't agree and still asked us to put money into the big bank.

God is essentially asking us for the same thing. The big bank is called heaven. And while those investments are paying high interest rates, heaven doesn't send out monthly statements. But how then can we prudently invest and measure our investments of time, money, talents, and so on?

All the mathematically motivated minds want to use numbers. And it's great to feed fifty hungry people, but how can you compare that to telling one person the gospel of Christ?

All the emotionally compelled people want to use their feelings. And it feels awesome to give children Christmas presents, but how can you compare that to giving money for international radio ministry?

Here are two simple principles that may help.

Principle 1: "We are ambassadors for Christ . . . we implore you on Christ's behalf, be reconciled to God" (2 Corinthians 5:20).

Let's say organizations A and B both feed hungry children in the inner city closest to where you live. Organization A is a multimillion-dollar corporation with a lot of experience. Organization B is smaller but financially well-run, and they purposefully teach the children about Jesus and how to have a personal relationship with the Bread of Life.

Which organization would be better to support as a steward?

Nice people can do nice things. But only Christ's people can be Christ's ambassadors and fellow workers (1 Corinthians 3:9). And that is what we are.

So when we choose to invest anything, we should make sure that ministry or Bible study or service project is compelled by the love of Christ and pursued in the truth of His counsel (the Bible). In this way we can be sure our money, time, and efforts are being spent on things that will last for eternity.

Principle 2: Count the cost (Luke 14:28).

This begins in prayer. Ask God for wisdom (James 1:5), and then pray as you review your budget, your schedule, and your skill set. Ask Him to show you where money may be saved, time may be reclaimed, and skills utilized.

Here are some ways I have found to be a wise steward (and I am still learning):

- Pack a sack lunch for work.
- Shop secondhand. (This is more fun, and you can purchase things for your church, local homeless shelter, crisis pregnancy center, and other ministries.)
- Cut back on entertainment.
- Read fewer novels or shorter ones.
- Take opportunities to serve with skilled individuals and learn from them.
- Make sure you are getting enough sleep to serve fully (this also includes eating well and exercising).

There are many ways to be a wise steward, so your list will look different than the one above. Don't worry if my list doesn't resonate with you.

There is a lot that comes into play when counting the cost. But it always ends the same way it starts: in prayer. Before saying yes, ask God if this is an opportunity He wants you to take, and then follow Him wherever He leads.

We are never alone in our
service or stewardship.

We may be single and have a single purpose, but we are never alone in our service or stewardship. As you likely noticed, prudent use of our stuff is less about calculating how to best increase our storehouse of eternal treasures in heaven and more about learning to obey the voice of God, who instructs and guides in the way we should go (Psalm 32:8). After all, He is the greatest eternal treasure.

REFLECT

Consider what opportunities God has given you. Where might you be able to steward your money and time better so you can more fully engage in God's purposes for you? How could you increase your skills to better serve others?

PRAY

Ask God to guide in the everyday moments of your life and give you a heart to hear and follow Him wherever He leads.

TAKE A SINGLE STEP

Pull out a piece of paper and write down where you are spending your time. Make one change to increase your availability to serve God.

Confession 30

THE PROTESTANT NUN— SAYING "YES" TO "NO"

YOU CAN KEEP A SECRET, right? If you can, keep reading, and if not, keep reading and then forget everything in this paragraph. I once prayed to get married to a specific man within a year. No joke. I asked God one September to make me this man's wife by next September. And guess what? The man got married within the year . . . but not to me.

I don't think I have ever gotten a cleaner, more obvious "no" to any prayer before or since. It has always puzzled me when I see or hear people complain, "God doesn't answer my prayers," because I know what I mean when I use those words. I mean I am not getting the answer I want.

We know God hears our prayers (1 John 5:14–15) and is faithful to answer. Even though it may not be what we want to hear, "no" is an answer. And so is "not now." When we don't like someone's answer, we think they didn't understand our question and ask again in a different way or with more information.

And this is what we do with God—albeit in a more disguised way. When we are dissatisfied with God's answers, we can't argue that He doesn't understand, so we tend to simply say He ignored us. But God is not ignoring us or disregarding our requests. God is answering our prayers. He always answers our prayers. God answered my prayer. He just said no.

Once we come to a place where we are able to recognize God's answer to a prayer, we have to be able to accept it. We have to internalize God's answer—yes, no, or otherwise—and respond with an unequivocal, "Yes, Lord."

We all know hearing "no" can be hard to make peace with, but there are answers that are even harder to accept. A "yes, but not the way you think" can be more difficult, because we then have to change our vision to fit God's. It can be challenging to deal with the uncertainty of "not now" and even more humbling to deal with the certainty of "wait."

But if "wait" is our answer, perhaps it's like being a Protestant nun. Yep, serious question now: Have you ever seen a Protestant nun?

My guess is you have. You may even have one in your family. You just didn't know it. In fact, a Protestant nun may not even know she is one. Okay . . . I hear crickets.

Catholic nuns and monks are immediately recognizable because of their clothes. These men and women have purposefully sacrificed their right to get married. They have dedicated their lives to the service of Jesus Christ and sealed it with vows and a ceremony.

Protestants don't do this. But if we are committed to following Jesus wherever He leads, we have dedicated our lives to His service. And we have given God our rights, including the right to get married. The Protestant nun is simply the Christian woman who lives contentedly and never marries. But until she dies, no one knows for sure she was a nun.

Monks and nuns know up front they will never get married—that's the deal. But all a Protestant nun knows is God might give back the right to get married or He might not, and whether she marries or not is up to Him.

I think a lot of us could make peace with a straight up "no." But that is not the way life (or God) works. The righteous live by faith. We do not get a road map or a checklist or anything resembling a plan when we sign up to follow Jesus. We get a gift of faith (Romans 12:3) and a Friend who never leaves (Proverbs 18:24).

Missionary and author Elisabeth Elliot, in her book *Keep a Quiet Heart*, contends that "the secret is Christ in me, not me in a different set of circumstances."[1]

That Christ is the one answering your prayers makes saying "yes, Lord. Thank You" possible, even when the answer is (or will eventually be) no.

At least it's not like we are the only ones who have ever been told no. Paul always had his thorn in the flesh. Moses was barred from the promised land. David's son died. And even Jesus still had to go to the cross.

Just because God says no doesn't mean He is angry or displeased with a request. I believe God is pleased with our desires to marry and raise families. After all, He knows who wired us this way. But God still might say no. I even think He was pleased with my choice in the specific man I prayed to marry way back when. And that answer was definitely no.

It is similar to a parent who tells their child they cannot go help with church cleanup because they need to do their homework. The parent was pleased with the activity and the desire to help, but something else was needed more at that moment. God is a good Father. He is motivated by love, not swayed by it. Meaning, He loves us enough to say no and pursue a good greater than what we are able to see or understand (maybe until heaven).

In *Stepping Heavenward*, hymn writer Elizabeth Prentiss says, "If God chooses quite another lot for you, you may be sure that He sees that you need something totally different from what you want."[2]

So just because God says no doesn't mean He is angry or punishing you—it may be just the opposite. Jon Bloom, cofounder of Desiring God, says in his article "The Unexpected Answers of God," "With regard to God's answers to prayer, expect the unexpected. Most of the greatest gifts and deepest joys that God gives us come wrapped in painful packages."[3]

Consider Elizabeth, a godly woman and wife (Luke 1:5–25). Luke goes out of his way to tell us both she and her husband walked with God blamelessly. But she was still barren. God was pleased with her desire for children. He was honored through her life and choices, but for many years the answer to her prayers was the same. God wasn't punishing, though He was patiently refining and actively instructing her faith. He wasn't angry. But the answer was still no . . . until it was "Yes!"

Zacharias was called to duty in the temple and given the privilege of burning incense to God in the holy of holies. This portion of the temple was entered into once a year. This portion of the temple was where the ark of the covenant rested, guarded by golden, heavenly warriors (2 Chronicles 5:7). By divine decree (Leviticus 16:29–34), the priest was to enter the Most Holy Place only once a year because above the mercy seat hovered the very Presence of God (Leviticus 16:2).

In this fearsome place (how often does God meet us in a fearsome place?), Gabriel—the angel of the Lord—delivered the news: Elizabeth would conceive and bear a son.

"What?!" I can picture Zacharias hyperventilating. "Elizabeth is too old to have a child! Her body has never been able to carry a baby!"

Gabriel was probably mystified. Why would this be a problem? We are talking about God. And thus, John the Baptist was born into this world.

But what if God never says yes to us? What if the answer is always going to be no?

Another way of saying this might be, What if we never get what we want?

If you had known me a few decades ago, you would have known I had a pretty intense sweet tooth, inherited from my grandmother. And while I never got to eat all the candy I wanted, one day in the 1930s, my grandma spent all her lunch money on candy corn—pounds of it.

Guess which sweet she never liked again? That's because we know what we think we want, just not what we really want. Some of us think we want to eat icing straight out of the bag (another chapter to our family's lore). But in reality nearly all of us would rather not be sick.

Most of us believe we would be happier and more effective for God if we were married. But really, only our loving Savior knows the truth about how we can best serve Him. And thank God, He not only knows the truth, He also knows what we think we want versus what we really want, and He knows how to change what we want to what He wants.

Regardless of how God answers our prayers, we need to consistently remind ourselves of the truth.

God is not toying with us. He's not going to jerk the prize away at the last moment and leave us with nothing to show for our sacrifice and obedience. "For God is not unjust to forget your work and labor of love which you have shown toward His name" (Hebrews 6:10).

God Himself walks with us to empower us to walk worthy of Him. In Christ we are single but never alone (Hebrews 13:5). In fact, we are a living demonstration that mankind is designed for God alone—to love and serve Him supremely (1 Corinthians 7:32).

Now the challenge is thrown to us: How will we do this?

Every semester in college, I took one fun class: karate, parkour, and ballet. (Belly dancing was also offered, but no one needs to be seeing my belly.) These classes represent a couple of the ways a Christian single could choose to approach life.

The Karate Approach

My karate class was 85–90 percent male, and at least 20 percent were wrestlers. My instructor had a rule: everyone had to spar with everyone else. I'm not that big. Sparring with men who have a hundred pounds of muscle on you will give you a whole new appreciation for hand-to-hand combat.

Make no mistake—some seasons in life, maybe even most, are hand-to-hand combat. Single or not, we are constantly at war and often on multiple fronts. Lies of the world, sin, and Satan assail us on numerous sides. Threats press down on us and loom large in our imaginations (2 Corinthians 4:7–10). And inside ourselves is a battle that we, frankly, resent—that fight between the law of life and the law of sin. In Romans 7 Paul talks about this war as a fierce, ongoing battle between the part of us that desperately wants to please God and the part of us that just as desperately wants to please ourselves.

> Make no mistake—some seasons
> in life, maybe even most, are
> hand-to-hand combat.

Yes, life is a fight, and we have been called to prepare for combat. Strap on that armor and go in the strength of the Lord (Psalm 71:16) as a good soldier of Jesus Christ (2 Timothy 2:3). Brace up and be steadfast, always abounding in the work of the Lord (1 Corinthians 15:58 and Ephesians 6:14).

A karate single has done everything to stand fast and is daily at work in the trenches of spiritual warfare.

The karate approach is intense.

The Parkour Approach

Parkour, or free running, is interacting with your environment in creative and acrobatic ways. Parkour is exactly what it sounds like—a very athletic endeavor. Balance on that. Bound over this. Bounce off this and then that. And if you want, throw in a cool back flip and a wall run. Parkour is about living life to the fun extreme.

Life is a gift from God. As Christians, our lives reflect the joy of an ongoing and deepening relationship with Christ (John 17:3). Through this relationship, Brother Lawrence maintains, even the mundane aspects of life can be full of marvel and excitement because those daily chores have the potential to be enthusiastic displays of the joy of our salvation (Psalm 51:12).[4]

Yes, life is joyful, and we have been commanded to rejoice in the Lord always. Again, I say rejoice (Philippians 4:4). Celebrate the security and revel in the freedom of your salvation (Romans 8:2). Study and seek God in anticipation and admiration of His wonderful grace toward us, His unprofitable servants (Luke 17:10).

A parkour single lives with the joy of the Lord as their strength and daily expresses the mystery that Jesus came to save them—sinners without hope in the world (Ephesians 2:12).

The parkour approach is full of wonder.

The Ballet Approach

Unlike in my karate and parkour classes, there was not a single male participant in my ballet class, which was good because ballerinas in training don't look like ballerinas on stage. I don't naturally point my toes or keep my back straight. And I'm sorry, you want my leg up how high?! Ballet—like life—looks easy when done right. The flowing beauty appears effortless in the moment. But behind that moment are hundreds of hours of training and conditioning. It doesn't just happen.

Life is beautiful in its relationships, its opportunities, and its precious moments. But making those moments possible takes hard work and discipline. A Christian is instructed to make no provisions for sin or self (Romans 13:14), knowing God's grace is there to choose rightly. The call is to reject what I want (no matter how tantalizing it may seem) and, in His strength, say yes to God and His ways (Deuteronomy 8:6).

Yes, life is beautiful, and Christians get to preview this. Our calling is to lay aside the filthiness of our natural lives and receive the Word of God with meekness (James 1:21). Strive to walk properly, knowing time is short—the night is far spent and the day is at hand (Romans 13:11–13). It is almost time to dance in the presence of our King, forever.

To this end a ballet single is hard at work to present herself approved unto God (2 Timothy 2:15).

The ballet approach is highly disciplined.

The Karparlet Approach

Whether you'd describe this as the combination strategy or the well-equipped approach or the biblical battle plan, you would be correct. This tactical solution is based on Psalm 119:160, "The entirety of Your word is truth."

There is nothing wrong with the karate, the parkour, or the ballet approaches, but they are all incomplete. We strive to emulate our Savior in all things, neither overemphasizing nor ignoring anything. The Bible is God's life-strategy manual. We need not and should not restrict ourselves to a single tactic when He has given us an arsenal.

We are looking for that intense, wonderful, disciplined approach that reflects "the whole counsel of God" (Acts 20:27). One complete approach fights the good fight (1 Timothy 6:12), abounds in joy (Nehemiah 8:10), and disciplines our bodies and appetites (1 Corinthians 9:27). The *ka*rate + *par*kour + bal*let* approach = the karparlet approach.

There are days to fight, and they will be intense. There are joy-filled days, and they will be wonderful. And the mundane days will call for self-discipline. But no matter the day, we rest in the grace of God (Romans 5:15) to fight on when we are too discouraged

(1 Samuel 2:8), to bring the sacrifice of praise when we are too overwhelmed (Hebrews 13:15), to obey when we are too weak (Hebrews 4:16), and to walk joyfully in all the ways of the Lord every day of our crazy lives with the Word of God (Psalm 119:162).

The karparlet approach is complete.

For the Protestant nun, the karparlet approach is the one that will enable us to most fully grasp His vision and purpose for our lives. Ours is a high and noble calling (2 Thessalonians 1:11), and whether in triumph or in struggle, we know God never withholds any good thing from those who walk with Him (Psalm 84:11). On the contrary, we have not begun to taste or see or imagine what God has designed for us (1 Corinthians 2:9).

So whether God's final answer to our prayers is yes or no, may we join with the psalmist in declaring, "I delight to do Your will, O my God, and Your law is within my heart" (Psalm 40:8).

—— REFLECT ——

Which life approach do you naturally gravitate toward, and what does that tell you about yourself?

—— PRAY ——

Ask God for grace to accept all of His answers.

—— TAKE A SINGLE STEP ——

Today, thank God for ten different ways your singleness makes you effective for Christ's kingdom. If you can't think of ten right away, don't worry. Start a running list. It might take a little time, but with our good God being who He is, before you're done that list will be much longer than ten.

FINAL CONFESSIONS: TRUTHS ABOUT CHRISTIAN SINGLES AND SINGLEHOOD

1. Singles are simply unmarried, married people. (More bluntly, singles are simply people!)
2. Even though we have our struggles, just like everyone else, there is nothing inherently wrong with us.
3. Our relationship status does not directly correlate to our character, maturity, or spirituality.
4. Most of us have wanted to be both single and married at different points in life.
5. We are not always happy or always unhappy (but neither are married people).
6. Single or married, all Christians have the most important thing in common: a relationship with God through Jesus Christ.
7. Together all Christians fulfill the mission of going into all the world and making disciples.
8. Singleness is God's gift.
9. God intentionally made some of us single to strengthen and build up His church and His kingdom.
10. God will show us the right time to marry . . . if there is such a time, because in His masterful design, and by His all-sufficient grace, some of us will continue to be single, wholeheartedly dedicated to Christ and Christ alone.

🐦

Dear Single Sisters,

I hope you have been encouraged, uplifted, and challenged throughout this book. If you are still feeling alone and left out, I get it. But I want you to know these truths (because you won't always feel them):

1. You are loved (Jeremiah 31:3).
2. You are valuable (Luke 12:7).
3. God has given you a mission (Ephesians 2:10).
4. You have purpose (Revelation 5:9–10).
5. God has provided you a family—His church, the family of God (1 John 3:1).

My heart's desire for you, and my prayer for myself, is that as we move forward in our singleness, we embrace these things:

1. Reflecting the beauty of God's holiness (Psalm 29:2)
2. Living fulfilled (John 10:10)
3. Being fruitful (2 Peter 1:5–8)
4. Growing in maturity (2 Peter 1:9–11)
5. Jumping into God's plans wholeheartedly and without looking back (Psalm 40:4–8)

Can't wait to see you out there living God's will!
Alisha

🐦

Dear Church Family,

Whether you are married, single, or somewhere in between, if Jesus Christ is your Savior and you are following Him with your life, this letter is to you. Every Sunday people sit in the pews next to you. Some of these people feel like church misfits, useless and unwanted.[1] That's a problem because the church is God's family. And God's family is made up of people from every corner of the globe and every life circumstance—including spinsterhood.

So I am asking for your help. Not help pairing up all the singles, but help encouraging them to live patiently, trusting and serving Jesus wholeheartedly. Don't just lock us away in an attic or a back room until we get married . . . as fun as this sounds to all the introverts! We need you to remind us that we belong, we are part of the body, and we matter.

Include us. On purpose. We want to support you in your marriages and families, work alongside you, and cheer you on in God's calling for your life. But if singles are segregated from the body, we feel isolated.

Invite us in. Specifically. You, like me, have spiritual gifts to build up the church. Our gifts are different, but together we are the body of Christ. United we can change the culture of our churches to welcome our single members, value their strengths, and more fully obey our mission to "go and make disciples."

Remember: God actually made us to be this way (maybe not forever, but certainly for right now). Our singleness allows us to focus on Christ without distraction and fully invest our lives into His kingdom.

I love you all and pray these confessions will help you see yourself correctly, view others from a spiritual perspective, and catch a vision for how God wants to use you.

Together, we are in Christ and living for His glory.

Alisha

NOTES

Confession 3: The Unloved

1. Jane Austen, *The Complete Novels of Jane Austen* (Hertfordshire, England: Wordsworth Editions, 2005), 235.
2. *Becoming Warren Buffett*, directed by Peter Kunhardt (New York: HBO, 2017), https://www.youtube.com/watch?v=PB5krSvFAPY.
3. Sinclair Ferguson, *Discovering God's Will* (Carlisle, PA: Banner of Truth, 2013), 92.

Confession 7: The Ring

1. John Eldredge and Stasi Eldredge, *Captivating: Unveiling the Mystery of a Woman's Soul* (Nashville: Thomas Nelson, 2005), 28.

Confession 10: Patience, My First Love

1. Westminster Divines, *The Shorter Catechism with Scripture Proofs* (Carlisle, PA: Banner of Truth, 2015), 1.
2. Brother Lawrence, *The Practice of the Presence of God* (Springdale, PA: Whitaker House, 1982), 53.
3. Lawrence, *Practice of the Presence of God*, 34.

Confession 12: Held in Honor

1. Jane Austen, *The Complete Novels of Jane Austen* (Hertfordshire, England: Wordsworth Editions, 2005), 822.
2. Dennis Rainey, "Building a Spiritual Foundation for Your Marriage,"

FamilyLife, accessed November 9, 2022, https://www.familylife.com
/articles/topics/marriage/staying-married/growing-spiritually/build
ing-a-spiritual-foundation-for-your-marriage.

3. Rob Jackson, "The Sexual-Spiritual Union of a Man and Woman,"
Focus on the Family, January 1, 2004, https://www.focusonthefamily
.com/marriage/the-sexual-spiritual-union-of-a-man-and-woman.

Confession 13: A Unicorn Among Horses

1. Martin Luther, as quoted in Jim Daly with Paul Batura, "Three Things
Martin Luther Teaches Us About Marriage," *Daly Focus* at Focus on
the Family, October 18, 2017, https://jimdaly.focusonthefamily.com
/Three-Things-Martin-Luther-Teaches-Us-Marriage.

2. Tony Evans, "Christian Singlehood," The Urban Alternative, accessed November 11, 2022, https://tonyevans.org/tony-evans-chris
tian-singlehood.

Confession 14: Made for This

1. Subby Sztersky, "Why Is There No Marriage in Heaven?" Focus on
the Family, accessed December 29, 2022, https://www.focusonthe
family.ca/content/why-is-there-no-marriage-in-heaven.

Confession 17: Jane's Horn

1. Jane Austen, *The Complete Novels of Jane Austen* (Hertfordshire,
England: Wordsworth Editions, 2005), 250.

Confession 19: Did She Really Just Ask That?! (Part 2)

1. Craig Denison, "Love God: It's All about Relationship," May 14,
2022, in *The First15 Podcast*, 3:38, https://first15devotional.libsyn
.com/love-god-its-all-about-relationship-1.

2. Lana Vrz, "God's Presence: The Importance of God in Marriage,"
Royal Wedding, February 27, 2020, https://www.officialroyalwed
ding2011.org/gods-presence-the-importance-of-god-in-marriage.

Confession 21: The Silly, Scary, and Sound—Advice on Getting Married

1. John Eldredge and Stasi Eldredge, *Captivating: Unveiling the Mystery of a Woman's Soul* (Nashville: Thomas Nelson, 2005), 216.

Confession 22: The "M" Word and a Few Friends

1. Steve Farrar, *King Me: What Every Son Wants and Needs from His Father* (Chicago: Moody, 2006), chap. 8.

2. Beth Ann Baus, "Why Do Women Turn to Pornography?," Crosswalk .com, January 10, 2022, https://www.crosswalk.com/faith/women /why-do-women-turn-to-pornography.html.

3. John Piper, "Missions and Masturbation," Desiring God, September 10, 1984, https://www.desiringgod.org/articles/missions-and-mastur bation.

Confession 23: The Other "M" Word

1. John Piper, "Battling the Unbelief of Lust," Desiring God, November 13, 1988, https://www.desiringgod.org/messages/battling-the-un belief-of-lust.

2. Craig von Buseck, "What Are the Three Parts of Man?," CBN, accessed November 11, 2022, https://www1.cbn.com/questions/what -are-the-three-parts-of-man.

3. *Porn Stats: 250+ Facts, Quotes, and Statistics About Pornography Use* (Owosso, MI: Covenant Eyes, 2018), 22, https://www.covenant eyes.com/e-books.

4. *Porn Stats*, 23.

5. Tim Challies, "Modesty Matters: The Heart of Modesty," Challies, November 12, 2013, https://www.challies.com/articles/modesty-mat ters-the-heart-of-modesty.

Confession 25: Surprised by Love

1. Angela Hunt, *The True Princess* (Waverly, PA: Lamplighter, 1992), 28.

Confession 27: Proverbs 31 Sermons

1. Melanie Chitwood, *What a Husband Needs from His Wife* (Eugene, OR: Harvest House, 2006), 71. Melanie formerly served with Proverbs 31 Ministries.

Confession 29: Single Purpose

1. Brother Lawrence, *The Practice of the Presence of God* (Springdale, PA: Whitaker House, 1982), 32.
2. Melanie Chitwood, *What a Husband Needs from His Wife* (Eugene, OR: Harvest House, 2006), 197.

Confession 30: The Protestant Nun—Saying "Yes" to "No"

1. Elisabeth Elliot, *Keep a Quiet Heart* (Ann Arbor, MI: Vine Books, 1995), 20.
2. Elizabeth Prentiss, *Stepping Heavenward* (Uhrichsville, OH: Barbour Books), 164.
3. Jon Bloom, "The Unexpected Answers of God," Desiring God, July 11, 2014, https://www.desiringgod.org/articles/the-unexpected-answers-of-god.
4. Brother Lawrence, *The Practice of the Presence of God* (Springdale, PA: Whitaker House, 1982), 25–26.

Final Confessions: Truths About Christian Singles and Singlehood

1. For more reading on singleness and the church, see Kristin Aune, *Single Women: Challenge to the Church?* (Milton Keynes, UK: Paternoster, 2002); Gina Dalfonzo, *One by One: Welcoming the Singles in Your Church* (Grand Rapids: Baker Books, 2017); Tony Evans, *Living Single* (Chicago, Moody, 2013); Katie Gaddini, *The Struggle to Stay: Why Single Evangelical Women Are Leaving the Church* (New York: Columbia University Press, 2022).